THE

PSALMS

IN

HAIKU

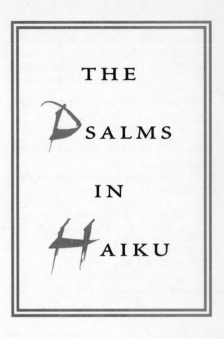

THE PSALMS IN HAIKU

Meditative Songs
of Prayer

Father Richard Gwyn

Seastone

BERKELEY, CALIFORNIA

Published by: Seastone, an imprint of Ulysses Press
               P.O. Box 3440
               Berkeley, CA 94703-3440

Library of Congress Cataloging-in-Publication Data

Gwyn, Richard.
    Psalms in haiku : meditative songs of prayer /
  by Father Richard Gwyn
      p. cm.
    ISBN 1-56975-096-3 (alk. paper)
    1. Bible. O.T. Psalms--Paraphrases, English.   I.
  Bible. O.T. Psalms. English.   II. Title.
  BS1440.G97 1997
  223'.205209--dc21   97-50453
                                                  CIP

ISBN: 1-56975-096-3

Printed in Canada by Transcontinental Printing

10 9 8 7 6 5 4 3 2 1

Editorial and production staff: David Wells, Lily Chou
Book Design: Sarah Levin, Leslie Henriques

Distributed in the United States by Publishers Group
West and in Canada by Raincoast Books.

Haiku is a Japanese form of lyric verse
having three unrhymed lines of five,
seven and five syllables.

This does not purport to be a learned work. It is, rather, something which could prove to be of interest and help to those who find the Psalms, as they are normally presented, beyond their intellectual and meditative scope. To them the simplicity – at times the starkness – of what I am now offering might well have greater appeal than would a daunting text with any learned footnotes.

My sources have been several versions I have immediately at hand: The Jerusalem Bible, 1966; The Revised English Bible, 1989; The New English Bible, 1982; The Grail Singing Version, Collins, 1981; with an occasional glance at Monsignor Ronald Knox's translation.

Richard Gwyn
December 1996

BOOK

ONE

How blessed is he
who rejects men's wicked ways
to follow God's law.

Unlike the wicked
he bears fruit in due season
prospering in peace.

Wind-blown chaff of sin
is no Judgement offering
to win approval.

God watches over
all who walk in honest paths;
He hates wickedness.

What is the meaning
of the shouting around us?
Threats against Yahweh.

Mocking at upstarts,
Yahweh strikes them with terror
and makes known His King.

"It is You, My Son,
and for this You were fathered;
ask Me what You will.

"The whole world is Yours.
Deal firmly with the peoples;
bend them to Your will."

Now see sense, you kings,
learn your lesson, you rulers;
bow down before God.

Never let His wrath
flare up and bring you to naught.
Find your joy in Him.

My enemies, Lord,
surround me, deny my right
to trust in Your love.

But You are my shield,
my glory, my sure support,
Who answer my prayer.

Peaceful is my sleep,
glad my waking to Your light.
My heart knows no fear.

To my rescue, Lord.
Strike down those who do evil
and save the upright.

You, Lord, the Victor.
May Your blessings ever rest
on all who serve You.

Answer, Lord, my cry.
You Who uphold all my rights.
In pity, hear me.

What is this sadness?
Why is your heart so heavy,
chaser of vain joys?

God performs wonders
on behalf of the faithful;
heeds when I call Him.

Give not way to sin;
pray in the depths of your heart
and at night be still.

The loyal man's gift
is a sacrificial heart
which trusts in Yahweh.

"Who will grant gladness?"
is our oft-repeated cry.
Shine on us, true Light.

The Giver of joy,
richer than corn and new wine
are You to my heart.

I lie down in peace
and in You alone, Yahweh,
rest secure in sleep.

4

5

Hear my sighs, Lord God.
Listen to my cry for help,
my King and my God.

I pray to You, Lord,
at daybreak present my case,
my eyes fixed on You.

No friend of evil,
no sinner finds Your favour,
pride quails at Your frown.

You hate men of sin,
bring liars to destruction,
and detest false hearts.

Great Your faithful love;
Your house and temple welcome
those who revere You.

In Your justice, Lord,
save me from my hidden foes;
set me on clear paths.

The lies of sinners
lead along seductive paths
to ruin and death.

Theirs the guilt, Lord God;
may their intrigues bring defeat,
a rebel's deserts.

For those who trust You
joy and endless hymns of praise,
beneath wings of love.

You bless the upright,
Your favour protecting them
as would a stout shield.

Lord, in Your anger
chide not nor punish my sins;
I crave Your pardon.

Heal my quaking bones,
cure my spirit to its depths;
How long, Lord, ... how long?

Relent and save me,
in Your great love rescue me
from Sheol's darkness.

The trap he digs deep
will open its mouth to him,
his spite's own victim.

My thanks to Yahweh.
I will sing praise to the name
of God the Most High.

Anger dims my eyes
at my foes' arrogant pride.
Grief gnaws at my heart.

Yahweh heeds my tears
and He, accepting my prayer,
will confound my foes!

In You I hide, Lord;
save me from the pursuers
who seek to harm me.

If I have done wrong,
if injustice or treason
call wrath down on me

may my foe take me,
trample my life to the ground
and crush me to dust.

Rise up in anger
against my arrogant foes;
give judgement, my God.

Let nations gather
before Your throne of judgement.
You alone are Judge.

Make clear to all, Lord,
my uprightness and honour;
break down their malice.

God Who is upright
is the shield protecting me
whose heart is honest.

Though slow to anger,
our just Judge ever threatens
the unrepentant.

When the enemy
whets his sword and draws his bow
his death is at hand.

His fire-tipped arrows
attest to his deep malice;
treachery his role.

Ruined are Your foes,
utterly crushed their cities,
all thought of them gone.

Yahweh is enthroned;
judging the world in fairness
He proclaims justice.

8

Yahweh, holy Lord,
how majestic is Your name
throughout all the world.

He who keeps singing –
even through the mouths of babes –
Your high majesty,

to him You give strength
to overcome the rebels
who rise against You.

I gaze on heaven,
the work of Your mighty hand,
at the moon and stars ...

What is frail mankind
that You think of Adam's son,
show Your care for him?

Yet You have crowned him
with almost godlike glory,
robed him with power.

You subject to him
wild beasts and tame, birds and fish –
make him lord of earth!

Yahweh, holy Lord,
how majestic is Your name
throughout the whole world.

I thank You, Yahweh;
with joyful heart I recount
all Your great wonders.

Strike them with terror;
Your judgement in my favour
throws them to the ground.

In time of trouble
may the Lord be a stronghold
for all the oppressed!

Rebuking nations,
destroying wicked people,
You blot out their name.

They can trust in You
who revere Your holy name,
for You stand by them.

Sing praise to Yahweh
Who dwells with us in Zion;
tell of His great deeds.

He never ignores
the cry of the afflicted;
He will avenge them.

Have pity on me;
Yahweh, see my affliction,
save me from the grave

that I may recount
Your praises at Zion's gates,
tell how You saved me.

Into their own trap,
into carefully laid snares
nations have fallen.

Making Himself known
Yahweh has, by His judgement,
ensnared the wicked.

May they be thrust down,
nations forgetful of God,
into Sheol's depths.

Arise, O Yahweh,
the strength of nations is naught
at Your judgement seat.

Making Himself known
Yahweh has, by His judgement,
ensnared the wicked.

Why so distant, Lord?
Why are You hiding away
in time of trouble?

Proud and wicked men
lay hold on the man in need,
seeking to trap him.

Puffed up with vain thoughts,
in their greed they mock the Lord
with blasphemous words.

Their hearts and minds closed,
the wicked arrogantly
turn their backs on God.

They think in their hearts
"We will never be shaken;
our future's assured!"

They beat down the poor
through deceit and oppression;
a constant menace.

They lie in ambush
to seize on such hapless prey
as fall to their wiles.

"God forgets!" they cry;
"not wishing to see the end,
He covers His eyes."

Lift up Your hand, Lord.
Why should the wicked spurn You
and deny Your might?

Your eyes are not blind
to the troubles of the poor;
You will play Your part.

The poor look to You;
You are their only Helper.
Cast down the wicked.

Root out all evil,
banishing it from the earth
and blotting it out.

You, Lord, heed the poor;
give them courage in sorrow,
listen to their moans.

Render fair judgement
for orphans and exploited;
free them from terror.

Yahweh our refuge;
so why are you urging us:
"Bird, flee to your hills?"

The wicked take aim,
their arrows fly through darkness
bring down honest men.

"If foundations fall,
how can even upright men
rebuild the ruins?"

God in His temple,
Yahweh gazing on His world,
keeping watch on men.

Yahweh observes all,
but turns away in anger
from violent men.

On them He will rain
red hot coals, fire and sulphur,
and breathe scorching winds.

Yahweh is upright:
so upright and honest men
will gaze on His face.

11

Yahweh, be our help,
for all loyal hearts are gone;
faith has fled from them.

Friends lie to their friends
both, under smooth words, hiding
double-dealing hearts.

12

Make an end, O Lord,
of duplicity of heart
and of bragging tongues!

"In our tongues" they claim
"lies strength; our lips are allies
none can overcome!"

"Now will I arise
for the poor who are plundered,
the needy who groan.

"And I," adds the Lord,
"shall place them in that safety
for which their hearts long."

The word of the Lord
is an unalloyed promise
seven times refined.

God, our protector
guards us from all wicked men
who seek to harm us.

They will be scattered
amongst those children of men
who applaud evil.

How much longer, Lord,
will you be forgetting me?
How long hide from me?

How long must I know
anguish of soul, grief of heart
and fear of my foes?

Answer me, Yahweh,
lest I sleep the sleep of death,
crushed by enemies.

I count on Your love,
pledge of a joyous haven
where I shall praise You.

14

The heart of a fool
cries aloud, "There is no God.
Everything is vile."

God, from His heavens,
looks among the human race
for those who seek Him.

All have turned from Him,
corrupting all His children
who once loved goodness.

No one understands
how they feed on my people,
ignoring their Lord.

Fear will be their lot
since God the righteous One
is with the upright.

Mock if you so wish
the plans of the godly poor;
God is their refuge.

Israel's saviour:
God bringing home His people.
What joy for Jacob!

In Your tent, Yahweh,
set on Your holy mountain,
who can hope to dwell?

Any upright man,
truthful and of blameless life,
who controls his tongue,

15

who harms not his friend,
discredits not his neighbour,
and honours good men,

who stands by his word,
and seeks no dishonest gain.
None can do him harm.

16

Protect me, O Lord.
In You, God, I find refuge
and my true Comfort.

I take my delight
in good and noble people,
not in the godless.

My birthright? Yahweh,
Who alone holds me secure!
What more could I ask?

Him, my Counsellor,
I will never cease to bless
By day or by night.

My gaze riveted
unblinkingly on Yahweh,
nothing can shake me.

My heart rejoices,
my soul filled full of gladness,
my body is safe.

You will not cast off
nor abandon to Sheol
Your faithful servant.

Show me the pathway
leading to life and fullness:
joy for ever more.

Hear, O Lord, my plea,
spurn not my cry for justice,
listen to my prayer.

Vindicate me, Lord,
give judgement in my favour,
You Who judge justly.

You plumb my heart's depths
and, testing, find no evil,
my mouth free from sin.

Your words I treasure,
violence I have eschewed,
walking in Your ways.

I call upon You,
knowing You will answer me;
listen to my words.

Unfold to my eyes
the great wonder of Your love,
Help of the oppressed.

Hide beneath Your wings
him who is as dear to You
as sight to the eye.

Save me from the hands
of lovers of violence
closing in on me.

All compassion stilled
and mouthing arrogant words
they surge towards me.

Like hungry lions
crouching to spring on their prey,
the enemy waits.

Arise, confront them;
bring them down, Lord, and save me;
Smite them with Your sword.

Make an end of them;
thrust them, Lord, out of this world.
Take them from this life.

May those whom You love
see their children satisfied;
to them leave their wealth.

I, in my justice,
ask only to see Your face –
waking to glory.

I love You, Yahweh,
Who save me from violence;
my Saviour, my Strength.

God, my lofty crag,
my fortress, my champion
where I find shelter.

You, Lord, are my shield,
and my surest defender,
my mighty tower.

I call on Yahweh,
to Whom all praise be given;
with Him I am safe.

Death all around me,
my life threatened by torrents,
hell lying in wait.

In anguish of heart
I cried to my God for help;
my cry reached His ears.

The earth shook and quaked,
mountains' foundations shuddered,
rent by God's anger.

Smoke from His nostrils,
from His mouth devouring flames;
glowing, searing heat.

Rending the heavens,
a storm-cloud under His feet,
Yahweh came to earth.

Borne by a cherub
on the wings of heaven's winds,
down to earth He swooped.

Enrobed in darkness,
His pavilion dark waters
and enfolding clouds.

Thick clouds coming forth
from enveloping splendour:
hail and glowing coals.

Yahweh's thund'rous voice,
the voice of the Lord Most High
fell upon all ears.

He loosed His arrows,
scattering them far and wide
and hurled forth lightning.

Springs of oceans bared,
the blast of His wrath revealed
the earth's foundations.

He reached from on high
and powerfully plucked me
from the raging sea.

He delivered me
from the grasp of enemies
strong beyond my strength.

They confronted me
in the hour of my peril
but God was with me.

He delivered me,
setting me utterly free
because He loved me.

The Lord remembered
my uprightness in His sight
and He repaid me.

His laws I have kept,
never turning from His paths
into evil ways.

Mindful of His word,
it has ever been my aim
to follow His law.

I have always sought
to be blameless in His sight,
to keep clear of sin.

Now the Lord rewards
as righteousness deserves
my virtuous ways.

To His faithful friends
the Lord shows Himself faithful,
kind to the blameless.

To those who are pure
You are pure; but the perverse
outdo in cunning.

You bring the humble
to safety; the arrogant
you cast to the ground.

You make bright my lamp;
Lord, You dispel the darkness
and light up my life.

My trust is in God:
with Him I can storm ramparts,
scale the highest wall.

God's way is blameless,
the Lord's word has stood the test,
He alone our shield.

Who, then, is Yahweh?
Is there any God like Him?
He is our firm rock.

He girds me with strength,
sweeping dangers from my path;
I, fleet as a deer,

am safe on the heights;
He trains my hands for battle,
to bend bows of bronze.

Shield of salvation
have You put into my hands;
Your arm sustains me.

Directing my steps,
You keep my feet from stumbling,
do not let me slip.

I pursue my foes,
throw down, make an end of them
before turning back.

Hurled down to the ground
they lie prone beneath my feet
and cannot arise.

You granted me strength
to cast down my assailants,
bowed them beneath me.

You have set my feet
upon the necks of my foes,
crushed those who hate me.

They cry to the Lord,
but there is none to save them;
God hears not their voice.

Dust before the wind
are the enemies I struck,
trampled underfoot.

I have been set free
from people who challenged me;
am now their ruler.

They hear and obey;
aliens cringe before me,
lose heart, and submit.

Then, grown faint of heart,
foreigners from their strongholds
come stumbling in fear.

The Lord our God lives;
hail, God of my salvation.
Blessed be my rock.

You put nations, Lord,
in subjection under me,
granting me vengeance.

You free me from foes,
set me over assailants
and violent men.

I proclaim You, Lord,
to the nations of the world,
sing praise to Your name.

You Who save the king,
keep faith with Your anointed,
David's lasting line.

Let heaven proclaim
the great glory of Yahweh
and make known His deeds.

Day speaks unto day,
night to night imparts knowledge
in utter silence.

God's designs go forth
to all corners of the earth,
scattered through the world.

From heavenly tent,
like a bridegroom filled with joy
the sun runs its course.

From one horizon
it journeys to the other
giving forth its heat.

Yahweh's perfect law
gives refreshment to the soul,
makes the simple wise.

The Lord's law is just,
and, enlightening the eyes,
gives joy to the heart.

The fear of the Lord
unsullied and enduring,
His commandments true.

More to be desired
than even the purest gold,
sweeter than honey.

19

They serve as warnings;
faithful in their observance
rich are our rewards.

Who can know our faults?
Grant, Lord, that we be wholly
   cleansed
from our hidden sins.

Guard Your servant, Lord,
from whatever smacks of pride,
free me from my sins.

May my every word,
every whisper of my heart
praise my Redeemer.

In time of trouble
may Jacob's God be for you
a tower of strength.

From His holy place
may He come to protect you,
bring help from Zion.

May He remember
your proffered sacrifices,
recall your praises.

May the Lord Yahweh,
aware of your heart's desires,
fulfil all your plans.

We acclaim with joy
victories won in God's name;
He heeds all your prayers.

Now I know that God
has heard His anointed One,
answers from heaven.

Some there are who trust
in horses and chariots;
our trust is in God.

They collapse and fall
while we rise up and stand firm.
The Lord hears and saves.

21

In Your strength, O Lord,
and at Your great victory,
the king rejoices.

You have heard his plea,
given him that which his heart
most greatly desires.

Bearing rich blessings,
You have set upon his head
a crown of pure gold.

He asked of You life
and to him You have given
never-ending days.

Great is the glory
with which You invested him,
wide his dominion.

You have arrayed him
with everlasting blessings,
joy in Your presence.

The king puts his trust
in the steadfast love of God
and shall not be moved.

His hand will reach out
to grasp all his enemies,
all those who hate him.

At Your appearing
blazing flames will consume them,
as the Lord commands.

Their offspring destroyed,
no longer will their children
encumber the earth.

The evil they planned,
plots aimed at bringing You low
could never prevail.

Before You they flee,
their heads running with the blood
set free by Your bow.

Rise, Lord, by Your might.
We shall sing a psalm of praise
honouring Your strength.

My God, O my God,
why have You forsaken me?
Do naught to save me?

I call You by day
but You, God, do not answer.
My nights know no rest.

Yet You are holy;
the praises of Israel
encircle Your throne.

In You our fathers
put their utmost confidence;
and You set them free.

They called on Your help
and were not disappointed:
You came to save them.

But I am a worm;
I, despised by the people
as less than human.

All who see me jeer;
mocking me they wag their heads,
mouthing their insults.

"He trusted in God,
so let God Who delights him
come to his rescue."

Who but You, O God,
took me from my mother's womb,
laid me on her breast?

To You, from my birth,
from my mother's very womb,
was I committed.

Now, in my distress,
do not abandon me, Lord.
Draw near and help me.

Hemmed in by wild bulls
that rend and roar like lions
where am I to turn?

My limbs like water
and all my bones disjointed,
my heart is but wax.

My throat is burning
as though full of scalding clay,
my jaws grip my tongue.

Dogs and evil men
beset me on every side,
tearing hands and feet.

My gaunt frame jeered at,
my garments gloated over,
lots cast for my robe.

Do not stand by, Lord.
My Strength, hasten to help me.
Save me from the sword.

From the axe shield me,
save my life from lions' jaws
and horns of wild bulls.

To all my brethren
seated in full assembly
I shall praise Your name.

May Jacob's whole race,
all the tribes of Israel,
praise His holy name!

He, far from scorning
the poverty of the poor,
hastened to help him.

It is to You, Lord,
that, in the Great Assembly,
I lift up my praise.

My vows I fulfil
in the sight of honest men
who walk in Your fear.

The poor will receive
whatever food they ask for,
far beyond their needs.

All who seek Yahweh
let them ever praise His name.
Long life to their hearts!

At the thought of Him
may all the ends of the earth
return to the Lord.

Let all families
and all nations of the world
bow down before Him.

For it is to Him
that kingly power belongs;
all nations are His.

For Him shall I live,
my descendants shall serve Him
for ages to come.

All generations
will speak of His mighty deeds:
all that He has done.

23

The Lord my Shepherd,
there is nothing I shall want,
grazing in His fields.

To quiet waters
He leads me; and as I rest
He revives my soul.

By paths of virtue
He, for the sake of His name,
lovingly leads me.

Even in darkness
no evil will befall me,
no harm do I fear.

Your rod and Your staff
will be of comfort to me,
signs of Your nearness.

In sight of my foes
You set me at Your table,
offer me choice foods.

You anoint my head
with the richness of Your oils.
My cup brims over.

Oh, how much goodness!
You pursue me with kindness
each day of my life.

Thus shall it be, Lord:
my home, the house of Yahweh
as long as I live!

To the Lord belongs
the earth and all it contains,
man and beast alike.

He Himself planned it,
set it upon the ocean,
firm upon the sea.

To whom has the Lord
granted the right to ascend
His holy mountain?

To whom the honour
of standing in His presence
in that holy place?

To all with clean hands –
of pure heart, too, and whose soul
turns away from sin.

Them Yahweh will bless.
The Saviour's vindication
will be their reward.

So it is with those
whose minds are set on seeking
the God of Jacob.

Gates, lift high your heads,
happily making welcome
the King of glory!

Who is he, this King?
Yahweh the strong, the valiant;
mighty in battle.

Gates raise high your heads,
give Him entrance, ancient doors –
our King of glory!

Who then is this King?
He is Yahweh Sabaoth,
Mighty Lord of Hosts.

Unto You alone,
Who are my Lord and my God,
I lift up my soul.

In You do I trust;
let me not be put to shame,
my foes mocking me.

Those who hope in You
shall not be disappointed
as are the faithless.

I count on You, Lord,
to make known to me Your ways,
to teach me Your paths.

May I never stray
from the truth of Your teaching,
O God my Saviour.

All my days are filled
with the hope I place in You
for You, Lord, are good.

Remember, O Lord,
the kindness and the mercy
You have always shown.

Do not remember
the sins of my younger days;
think of me with love.

Yahweh is upright,
ready to lead in his ways
even poor sinners.

The humble and poor
He leads to righteousness –
guides their every step.

The ways of the Lord
are, for those who keeps His law,
bright with love and truth.

Lord, forgive my guilt
for the honour of Your Name,
great though that guilt is.

To one who fears Him
the Lord Himself will point out
the way he should choose.

To him will He give
both lasting prosperity
and land for his sons.

The Lord grants friendship
and reveals His covenant
to His faithful friends.

My eyes ever fixed
on Him Who rescues my feet
from snares of evil.

Turn Your eyes to me
who am lonely and oppressed;
show me Your favours.

Soothe my heart's anguish
and free me from the distress
brought upon myself.

See my affliction
and the toil that besets me.
Take away my sins.

Many are my foes
and violent the hatred
they show towards me.

Come to my defence
that I may never be mocked
for my trust in You.

May integrity
and my uprightness of heart
be my protection.

My hope is in You,
Who will redeem Israel
from all its sorrows.

26

Give me justice, Lord,
for my life has been blameless
and in You I trust.

Examine me, Lord;
O test my heart and my mind;
put me to the proof

for Your constant love
is ever before my eyes;
I live in Your truth.

Never with wastrels
have I associated,
nor with hypocrites.

Doers of evil
I have always avoided;
their ways disgust me.

Washed free from all guilt
I join in the procession
around Your altar.

I make known Your deeds,
with thankful heart, praising You,
telling Your wonders.

How greatly I love
the house wherein You dwell, Lord,
bright with Your glory.

Never cast me forth
with sinners and men of blood.
Sweep me not away.

Do not count me, Lord,
among men of blood and greed,
doers of evil.

I, for my part, Lord,
walk the path of perfection,
my feet on firm ground.

I find happiness
in blessing Your holy name
in the assembly.

27

The Lord is my light
and He is my salvation;
whom then shall I fear?

He is my stronghold;
there is no one I need dread
while He upholds me.

Evil men draw near
to bring trouble upon me;
but they themselves fall.

My heart would not fear
even were I surrounded
by bands of armed men.

Should war threaten me
I will remain unafraid,
for still would I trust.

Just one thing, O Lord,
shall I go on asking for
with a longing heart:

to live in Your house,
the very house of the Lord,
throughout my whole life,

there to gaze upon
the glory of His beauty
within His temple.

He will keep me safe
sheltering under His roof
in times of evil.

He will conceal me
in the shadow of His tent,
safe from misfortune.

My head will be raised
in sight of the enemies
who encircle me,

and I shall offer
an exultant sacrifice
within the Lord's tent.

I will sing with joy,
make music to the Lord's name,
singing psalms of praise.

Hear my voice, O Lord,
give answer when I call You,
showing me mercy.

"Come," my heart has said,
"seek the presence of Your Lord."
I seek Your face, Lord.

Do not hide from me
nor turn away in anger
from Your servant, Lord.

You Who have helped me,
do not now abandon me,
O God, my Saviour.

Should my own father
and my mother reject me,
You, Lord, would help me.

Teach me Your way, Lord;
let not my enemies' greed
hinder my advance.

Lead me by smooth paths,
safe from the lies and falsehood
of furious foes.

I firmly believe
I shall see my Lord's goodness
in the world to come.

Hope then in the Lord;
let your heart be strong and brave.
Hold firm to the end.

To You, Lord, I call;
do not be deaf to my cry,
O Rock Who gives strength.

If You are silent
I shall go down to the pit,
into the abyss.

Listen to the plea
I am bringing before You
at Your holy shrine.

Drag me not away
with scheming ungodly men
who veil their malice.

They should be repaid
as their wickedness deserves,
the work of their hands.

They fail to discern
the mighty works of the Lord,
and ignore His deeds.

May they be dealt with
according to their deserts
and never pardoned.

Blessed be the Lord.
In His goodness He has heard
my plea for mercy.

The Lord is my Strength,
He alone my saving shield.
In Him my heart trusts.

By Him was I helped;
lifting up my voice in song,
my heart leaps for joy.

Strength of His people,
the Lord is a sure refuge
for His anointed.

Save Your people, Lord,
bless those who belong to You,
the sheep of Your flock.

Pay the Lord tribute,
hail His glory and power;
hail Him, sons of God.

Glory to His name,
worship in His holy court,
let us adore Him.

The voice of the Lord
echoes over the waters,
with might and power.

That voice of the Lord
across the fathomless deeps –
power and splendour!

The voice of the Lord
shakes the Lebanon cedars,
splintering their trunks.

He makes Lebanon
skip like a frolicsome calf
or a young wild ox.

The voice of the Lord
makes fiery flames burst forth,
shakes the wilderness.

The Lord's voice resounds
and Kadesh begins to writhe
as though in travail.

The voice of the Lord
sets terebinths shuddering,
stripping forests bare.

All in the temple
cry out "Glory" to the King
seated on the floods.

He, eternal King,
will give strength to His people
blessing them with peace.

I will praise You, Lord;
You have saved me from my foes,
You have rescued me.

To You I cried, Lord,
and because I sought Your help
You brought me healing.

Up from Sheol's depths
into which I was sinking
You, O Lord, plucked me.

Sing psalms to the Lord,
loyal servants who love Him;
give thanks to His name.

Fleeting is His wrath,
His favour lasts a lifetime,
turns weeping to joy.

"Nothing will shake me"
I said in the certainty
of Your kind favour.

Then You hid Your face
and my strong mountain trembled
as dismay gripped me.

I called out to You,
pleading with You for mercy,
for freedom from death.

What is to be gained
by my going to the grave?
Can dust give You praise?

Be kind to me, Lord,
pay heed to my urgent plea
and grant me Your help.

My sackcloth replaced
by robes of joy, my mourning
was turned to dancing.

I sing psalms to You
without ceasing, Lord my God,
in unending praise.

In You I shelter;
rescue me in Your goodness,
let me not be shamed.

Make haste to hear me.
Be, Lord, my rock of refuge,
stronghold of safety

You are my stronghold,
since You lead me and guide me
for Your own name's sake.

Keep my feet clear, Lord,
of nets that my enemies
set to entrap me.

Into Your hands, Lord,
I am entrusting myself,
since You redeemed me.

O Lord, God of truth,
You detest those who worship
false and worthless gods

My trust is in You:
gladdened by love unfailing,
in You I rejoice.

My wretchedness, Lord,
and all that afflicts my soul,
though clear in Your sight,

have not induced You
to hand me over to those
who seek to harm me.

No, You have set me
in a place of true freedom,
to go where I will.

Be gracious to me,
for I, Lord, am in distress,
my eyes dimmed by grief.

Sorrows bow me down;
my years burdened with sighing,
I stumble and fall.

All my strength is spent,
my bones are wasting away,
oppressors mock me.

I have become, Lord,
a thing to arouse contempt,
loathsome to neighbours.

When my friends see me
rather than acknowledge me,
they avert their gaze.

I am forgotten,
as though I were a dead man,
a thing thrown away.

Fear surrounds me
as the slander of the crowds
falls upon my head.

For all about me
are plotting to do me harm,
threatening my life.

But for my part, Lord,
all my trust is placed in You,
You, Who are my God.

I am in Your hands
and You alone can free me
from those who hate me.

With unfailing love
let Your face shine out again
on him who serves You.

Let him not be shamed
who calls to You for mercy,
but shame the wicked.

May they fall silent
in the graves prepared for them:
overcome at last.

Those lips stricken dumb
that once spoke against the just
with pride and contempt.

Great is the goodness
You manifest in mercy
to those who fear you;

that goodness You show
to those whose trust never fails
before mere mortals.

Your friends You conceal,
safe in Your holy presence,
from enemies' eyes.

You hide them away,
safe from the contentious tongues
of conspiracy.

Blessed be the Lord
Who showed me unfailing love
in time of great need.

In alarm I cried
"I am shut out from Your sight"
but You heard my cry.

Love the Lord, you saints,
for He protects the faithful
and rejects the proud.

Be strong, loyal friends;
raise high in courage those hearts
that hope in the Lord.

Happy is the one
whose fault has been forgiven,
is quite forgotten.

O happy indeed
all those whom the Lord finds free
of guilt and deceit.

32

While I kept silent
my bones were wasting away;
I groaned all day long.

By day and by night
Your hand lay heavy on me
and my heart was parched.

Then I found the strength
to acknowledge I had sinned,
to tell of my guilt.

As soon as I said
"I shall confess to the Lord"
You forgave my sin.

So should every heart
in times of anxiety
turn to You with trust.

Even should great floods
threaten to overwhelm them
they shall be unharmed.

The Lord is for me
a hiding-place from distress,
my sure salvation.

I will instruct you,
give you guidance and counsel,
keep you in My sight.

You must not behave
in the way of horse or mule,
unreasoning beasts.

Unless they are curbed
by means of bridle and bit
they will not approach.

While many sorrows
visit those who do evil,
love enfolds the just.

Rejoice and be glad,
sing praise, you righteous ones,
those of honest heart.

Shout for joy in God,
all you of righteous heart;
praise honours the good.

Give thanks to the Lord,
make music in His honour
with lyre and harp.

Sing Him a new song,
play aloud with all your skill,
shouting in triumph.

The word of the Lord
is ever to be trusted
and His works endure.

He is a lover
of right-thinking and justice.
His love fills the earth.

By His word were made
the heavens and their armies;
all at His command.

He brought together
the seas with all their waters
and stored up the deeps.

The fear of the Lord
should make the whole world tremble;
let all revere Him.

At the Lord's command
the earth came into being,
firm and unyielding.

The plans of nations
are frustrated by the Lord,
their plots overthrown.

The Lord's high purpose
will continue to stand firm
everlastingly.

How happy are those
who look on God as their Lord –
who are His people.

Gazing from His heights
the Lord sees all the nations,
the whole human race.

From His holy throne
every dweller on the earth
clearly seen by Him.

He fashions the heart
of every human being,
watching all their works.

A king is not saved
by the might of his army,
nor we by prowess.

How vain to entrust
our lives to a horse's strength;
that cannot save us.

The eyes of the Lord
are upon those who fear Him,
who hope in His love.

He can rescue them
from imminent threat of death,
even from famine.

Our soul waits for Him,
knowing that the Lord alone
is our help and shield.

Our hearts are joyful
because we have placed our trust
in His holy name.

Your unfailing love
ever remain, Lord, with us
whose hope is in You!

Ever and always
will the praise of the Lord's name
be upon my lips.

To Him give glory,
you who are humble of heart;
hearing Him, be glad.

Glorify the Lord;
let us be one in praising
His most holy name.

I sought the Lord's help;
and, hearing my petition,
He freed me from fear.

Faces turned to Him
become radiant with joy
and are never shamed.

This poor wretch cried out
from the depth of his troubles;
God heard and saved him.

His angel watches
over those who revere Him,
and He rescues them.

Taste, see for yourself
how good the Lord is to all
who count on His help.

You, His holy ones,
should hold him in holy fear;
He denies you nought.

Though even the strong
suffer want and go hungry,
you will lack nothing.

Come, children; hear Me
as I speak to you about
the fear of the Lord.

Which one among you
dreams of a prosperous life
enjoyed to the full?

Watch over your tongue,
never speak maliciously
and do not tell lies.

Shun what is evil
seeking always to do good;
thus will you know peace.

The eyes of the Lord
are upon the righteous,
His ears hear their cry.

The Lord sets His face
against those who do evil,
His mind closed to them.

Those who cry for help
are heard by the Lord and freed
from all their troubles.

He is close to those
whose courage is at an end
and saves crushed spirits.

Though the righteous
may know many misfortunes,
the Lord will save them.

The Lord will protect
every bone in their body;
none will be broken.

Their own wickedness
brings death to evil-doers
who hate what is good.

The Lord delivers
His own righteous servants,
spares those who seek Him.

Plead my cause, O Lord,
against all my enemies;
fight those who fight me.

Take up, I beg You,
buckler and shield against them
and come to my aid.

Brandish spear and axe
against those who pursue me,
O Lord, my Saviour.

May shame and disgrace
fall on those who are seeking
to cut short my life.

Let them be dispersed,
who make plans for my downfall,
blown about like chaff.

May the Lord's angel
drive them off and pursue them
through dark, slimy paths.

In sheer wantonness
they dug a pit for my feet,
snares to entrap me.

May they fall headlong
into the pit they have dug,
into their own snare.

Then shall I rejoice
in the Lord Who has saved me,
crying with full heart:

"Lord, who is like You,
Who free the weak from the strong
and save the oppressed?"

Liars take the stand
and accuse me unjustly
of imagined crimes.

Thus do they repay
my good deeds with their malice,
saddening my soul.

Yet, when they were ill
I spent my days in fasting,
that they might be cured.

I walked with bowed head,
grieving as for a brother,
worn out with mourning.

But when I stumbled
they hemmed me in joyfully,
tore me to pieces.

When I fell over
they mocked and derided me,
ground their teeth at me.

How much longer, Lord,
will You watch without helping?
Come to my rescue!

Then I shall praise You
before the great assembly,
praise You everywhere.

Let not lying foes
who hate me without reason
jeer at my downfall.

No lovers of peace,
they always seek to hatch plots
against the peaceful.

Their mouths wide open,
they shout against me, crying,
"We saw it ourselves?"

All this You have seen.
Do not, then, stay silent, Lord;
do not hold aloof.

Agree, Lord my God,
to be my vindicator,
stand up for my cause.

You are righteous,
so be my judge, Lord my God;
and stop their gloating.

Do not let them say,
"Yes, we have defeated him,
our case has been won."

May those rejoicing
at the sight of my downfall
themselves be disgraced.

May shame and dismay
be the lot of all who sought
my discomfiture.

But let there be joy
for those who upheld my cause
in sight of my foes.

Let them ever say,
"Great is the Lord Who delights
in His servant's peace!"

My tongue will declare
Your power and Your goodness
always, without end.

Sin, deep in their hearts,
whispers to all the wicked
who set God at naught.

They flatter themselves,
making no effort to change
from evil to good.

36

In their mouths are found
mischief and deceitfulness,
all wisdom has fled.

How to cause trouble
is their preoccupation,
the theme of their dreams.

So set are such men
on their wicked way of life,
nothing will change them.

Your limitless love
reaches, Lord, to the heavens,
Your faith to the skies.

Your righteousness,
like towering mountain peaks
touches the heavens.

Your judgements, O Lord,
go down to fathomless depths –
deeps ever unplumbed.

You give protection
to both man and beast, O Lord.
How precious Your love!

Gods and frail mortals
seek refuge in the shadow
of Your outspread wings.

Your bounty feeds them
and from Your pleasant rivers
You give them to drink.

For with You, O Lord,
is the true fountain of life
and Your light gives light.

Your unfailing love
remains with those who know You,
the honest of heart.

Let me not be crushed
by the feet of haughty men,
nor cast from Your sight.

How great is the fall
of all those who do evil!
Never shall they rise.

Doers of evil
should be no source of worry,
nor excite envy

for, like blades of grass,
they will soon wither away,
fade like green pasture.

37

Trusting in the Lord
and seeking to do His will
will bring you true peace.

Delight in the Lord
and you will be rewarded
with your heart's desire.

If, with total trust,
you commit yourself to Him
He will act in you.

Your righteousness
and your justice will shine out
with the sun's brightness.

Wait for Him in peace,
patiently, without envy
in quiet of heart.

Be angry no more,
have done with wrathful thinking
which leads to evil.

Doers of evil
will come to an evil end:
utterly destroyed.

Trust then in the Lord
and you will possess the land
promised to His friends.

In a little while
the wicked will be no more,
their place left empty.

Then shall the humble
receive their inheritance
and enjoy their wealth.

All the wicked plot
against the friends of the Lord,
gnash their teeth at them.

The Lord laughs at them
because He is well aware
that their time is short.

With their swords unsheathed
and their bows bent to the full
they threaten God's friends.

Those swords will pierce
the hearts of the attackers
and those bows broken.

The few possessions
of an honest man outweigh
the wicked man's wealth.

The Lord will uphold
the righteous, but will crush
those of wicked ways.

He keeps guard over
the good and their heritage
throughout all their days.

They shall not be shamed;
even in times of famine
they shall eat their fill.

Sinners will perish;
like fuel, and God's enemies
will go up in smoke.

Loans to the wicked
bring ruin on the lender;
the just give freely.

Those blessed by the Lord
will possess the land; the cursed
He will dispossess.

The Lord guides the steps,
taking joy in the progress,
of one whom He loves.

Though he should stumble
he will not fall to the ground;
the Lord holds him fast.

I, who am grown old,
never saw the good cast off,
nor their young starving.

God blesses the young
of all who are generous
in serving the poor.

Those who shun evil
and seek to do what is right
live in lasting peace.

The Lord loves justice
and He will never forsake
His loyal servants.

Those without the law
are banished from the Lord's sight,
their children cut off.

But the righteous
will come to possess the land,
for ever his own.

From the just man's mouth
there come forth words of wisdom,
and concern for all.

Reigning in his heart
is the mighty law of God;
his steps never fail.

Miscreants keep watch
on those who live honestly,
seeking to kill them.

Never will the Lord
allow them to be condemned
by wicked judges.

Wait then for the Lord;
if you strive to follow Him
you will be kept safe.

He will raise you up
and, the wicked once destroyed,
their land will be yours.

When destruction strikes,
you will be there to witness
what becomes of them.

I have gazed upon
wicked men like towering
Lebanon cedars.

Passing by again
I looked, but they were not there –
nowhere to be seen.

Not so for the good;
they are firmly established
and leave descendants.

Sinners are wiped out
and their descendants destroyed;
no more are they seen.

For the righteous,
deliverance comes from Him
Who is their refuge.

The Lord will help them,
keep them safe from the wicked.
He is their shelter.

Do not angrily
rebuke me, nor wrathfully
punish me, O Lord.

Deep have Your arrows
gone into me; Your hand weighs
heavy upon me.

My whole body aches
on account of Your anger;
my sins have scarred me.

My iniquities
tower high above my head;
too heavy to bear.

Great is my folly!
all my wounds are festering
and foul is their stench.

I am brought down low:
prostrate and, from morn to night,
like one in mourning.

Fever burns my loins,
and there is no wholesome flesh
on my mortal frame.

Battered and benumbed,
crushed with grief I groan aloud
in anguish of heart.

All my longing, Lord,
lies open before Your eyes,
my pain no secret.

My heart is throbbing,
my strength is utterly spent,
no light in my eyes.

Friends and companions
avoid me like a leper;
kinsfolk stand far off.

Those who seek my life
are laying their snares for me,
ever at their schemes.

I, like a deaf man,
hear nothing; like a dumb man
open not my mouth.

So do I behave:
like one who has no hearing,
one with no defence.

My hope, Lord my God,
is stayed upon Your defence
made on my behalf.

"Never allow them
to rejoice over me, Lord,
if my foot should slip."

I am on the brink
of disasters that threaten
and in constant pain.

I confess my guilt
and am forever troubled
because of my sin.

Many are my foes
for no cause that I gave them;
unprovoked hatred.

They plan to repay
good with evil, opposing
my good intentions.

Do not forsake me;
my God, do not stand far off.
Hasten to help me.

"I must be watchful,"
I said, "lest I give freedom
to my sin-prone tongue.

"Faced by wicked men,
I must not allow my lips
to give way to sin."

So I held my peace;
though my heart burned within me
I refrained from speech.

Then, as I pondered,
the fever within me grew
until words burst forth.

"Tell me, Lord, how long
will it be before I die –
how many days left?

"My time a mere span,
to You no more than a breath,
just a puff of wind.

"Man – fleeting shadow,
his wealth, dispersing vapours –
for whom the profit?"

Why am I waiting?
What can I expect, O Lord?
My hope is in You.

Free me from sinners
that I may no longer be
the plaything of fools.

39

I shall remain dumb,
nor shall I open my mouth
for You have done this.

Lay aside Your scourge;
I am exhausted by blows
raining upon me.

You punish man's sins,
rebuke and correct his faults
by harsh penalties.

His longings snuffed out,
mortal man sees that he is
but a puff of wind.

O Lord, hear my plea.
Turn to me and no longer
be deaf to my cry.

I am but a guest
seeking shelter in Your house,
as did my fathers.

Do not frown on me.
Make my heart rejoice again
before I go hence.

I awaited Him.
Suddenly He stooped to me –
the Lord heard my cry!

From the deadly pit
He has drawn me to Himself,
out of mud and clay.

40

My feet He has set
upon a rocky firmness,
steadying my steps.

Now He has taught me
a new song of praise to God,
put it on my lips.

Many, seeing this,
will be overcome with awe
and learn to trust Him.

How happy are those
who put their trust in the Lord
and avoid false gods.

How many wonders
You work for us, Lord my God,
how great Your designs.

No deeds can compare
with the wonders You have done –
and all for our good!

It would be my joy
to proclaim them far and wide
but my words fail me.

You seek no victim,
no offering other than
my attentive ear.

Here I am, I said,
my one wish to do Your will,
to observe Your law.

In the assembly
I have proclaimed what is right
with undisguised words.

"Never have I kept
Your justice hidden away
deep down in my heart.

Your love and Your truth
I have never kept hidden
in the assemblies.

I know that You, Lord,
will never withhold from me
Your loving kindness.

Evils beset me,
press upon me from all sides;
my sins smother me.

My very sight fails
and my heart sinks at the thought
of my countless sins.

Show me mercy, Lord;
come quickly to rescue me,
for I need Your help.

Put to confusion
those striving to cause me harm,
who seek to kill me.

Stop fast in their tracks
those trying to bring me down,
who jeer at my lot.

May all who love You
be full of joy and gladness
at Your great goodness.

All awaiting You,
who long for Your saving aid,
will sing Your glory.

I, wretched and poor,
urgently need Your help, Lord.
Come! Do not delay!

Happy is the man
who shows concern for others,
succouring their needs.

In time of trouble
the Lord will be at his side,
happy to help him.

Him the Lord protects,
granting him security
and the gift of life.

He will not be left
to the power of his foes
or their ill-treatment.

The Lord will be there
to help in his suffering,
to restore his health.

As for me, I said:
"O Lord, have mercy on me;
heal me who have sinned?"

"He is past curing"
my enemies say of me;
"may he soon be dead!"

They come to mock me,
hearts full of malicious thoughts
which they spread abroad.

All those who hate me
whisper around my bedside,
hoping for the worst.

41

"Evil spells" they say
"have been cast upon the man;
there can be no hope!"

The friend I trusted,
who so often shared my meals,
has turned against me.

Restore my health, Lord,
and grant that I may repay
their spite to the full.

Then shall I be sure
that You take delight in me,
thwarting all my foes.

Upheld by You, Lord,
forever in Your presence,
I shall rest unscathed.

Blessed be the Lord,
the great God of Israel,
For ever. Amen.

BOOK

TWO

Like the doe that longs
for running streams so, my Lord,
yearns my soul for You.

My soul is thirsting;
when can I enter and see
the face of my God?

Tears my only food
as, day and night, they ask me
"Where, then, is your God?"

In distress of soul
I call to mind how I marched
to the house of God.

The jubilant throng,
songs of joy and thanksgiving,
pilgrims wild with joy.

Yet I am cast down
and my soul grieves within me
as one without hope.

I will turn to God
Who alone is my Saviour;
I will praise Him still.

My very sadness
reawakens in my mind
thoughts of Your nearness

as at Jordan springs,
from the heights of Mount Hermon
or humbler Mizar.

Deep calls upon deep
in the roar of the waters;
Your waves engulf me.

As day succeeds day
the Lord is pleased to grant us
His unfailing love.

On my lips at night
is a song of prayerful praise
to Him Who gives life.

"Why, O God, my Rock,
have You put me from Your mind
and left me to mourn?"

My foes oppress me;
jeering, they taunt me and ask,
"Where then is your God?"

Deep my misery!
I am groaning in distress,
awaiting my God.

Put your hope in God.
I will praise Him at all times:
the God Who saves me.

God, uphold my cause
and give Your judgement for me
against the godless.

Save me, O my God,
from deceitful, cunning men.
Come to my rescue.

You are my shelter;
why do you abandon me
to my oppressors?

Send forth, Lord, Your light;
let Your truth serve as my guide
to Your holy hill.

Then at Your altar
I shall praise You on the harp,
God of my delight.

Deep in misery,
groaning in fearful distress,
still am I waiting.

I will wait for God
and constantly give him praise:
my God, my Saviour.

43

With our own ears, Lord,
we have heard from our fathers
tales of long ago.

The deeds You performed,
the mighty works of Your hand
in days long since gone.

44

Nations uprooted
to make way for our fathers;
great peoples laid low.

It was not their swords
that brought them such victories;
none of their doing.

It was Your right hand
and the splendour of Your face.
Your love was with them.

You, my King, my God,
gave victories to Jacob
and his followers.

We beat down our foes
and trampled our aggressors
by Your holy name.

Not trusting my bow
nor the sharpness of my sword,
I counted on You.

All who hated us
were overcome by Your might.
You conquered our foes.

Our boast was in You.
Ceaselessly we praised Your name,
and not without cause.

But now You scorn us.
No longer are You marching
side by side with us.

Our foes drive us back;
You let raiders attack us
whenever they wish.

Like sheep for slaughter
we are scattered far and wide
because You so willed.

Your people You sold
making nothing by the sale,
counting them worthless.

You have given us
to the contempt of neighbours –
taunters and mockers.

Among the nations
You have made us a byword,
butts for derision.

I, covered with shame,
am brooding throughout the day
in utter disgrace,

overwhelmed by taunts,
by insults and blasphemy
heaped on me by foes.

All this befell us
who had not forgotten You,
never betrayed You.

We had not turned back
or allowed our feet to stray
from paths of goodness.

Yet You have crushed us,
cast us into jackal's dens,
to darkness and death.

Had we turned from You
in favour of other gods,
would You not have known?

You can read our hearts,
know that for You we face death
as sheep face slaughter.

Bestir Yourself, Lord,
and no longer reject us.
Why are You sleeping?

Do not hide Your face,
heedless of our misery
and our suffering.

For Your love's sake, Lord,
arise and come to our help;
redeem and free us.

45

My heart overflows
with noble words for the king;
to him I must sing.

The song I have made
trips flowingly from my tongue,
as from a scribe's pen.

You are the fairest
of all the children of men
with grace on your lips.

Blest are you by God
with sword ready at your side,
O warrior king.

In splendour and state
you ride on triumphantly
in the cause of right.

Taut stretched your bowstring,
nations lie at your mercy
and your foes lose heart.

Eternal your throne
with the sceptre of justice,
pledge of your kingdom.

Your love for justice
and your hatred for evil –
win you God's favour.

With oil of gladness
He anoints you, setting you
above other kings.

Your rich robes fragrant
with scent of aloes and myrrh,
music welcomes you.

The daughters of kings
are your maidens of honour;
at your right, the queen.

Listen, O daughter,
hear and consider my words:
forget your people.

Forget your own home.
The king, won by your beauty,
he is now your lord.

Pay homage to him
and the richest of nations
will seek your favour.

The king's dear daughter
is clothed in robes embroidered
with pearls set in gold.

Virgins go with her
into the royal presence
with gladness and joy.

The sons born to you
will be rulers of the earth,
as were your fathers.

From age unto age
will your name be remembered
and your praises sung.

God is our refuge,
a timely help in trouble,
the Giver of strength.

Never shall we fear
even though mountains should fall
into ocean depths;

when wild waters rage
and mountains are washed by waves,
God is our stronghold.

Consider God's works
and the redoubtable deeds
He has done on earth:

He has stamped out wars,
breaking bows and snapping spears,
setting shields ablaze.

"Know that I am God,
supreme among the nations,
high above the earth!"

Yahweh Sabaoth,
the Lord of hosts, is with us.
Jacob's God, our shield.

Nations, clap your hands,
acclaiming the Lord your God
with shouts of delight.

Yahweh, the Most High,
it is He Whom we must dread,
Great King of the earth.

He brings the peoples
under our domination,
prostrate before us.

Our inheritance,
our glory, is from the Lord –
bestowed out of love.

To shouts of triumph
and a fanfare of trumpets
the Lord has gone up.

Sing praise to our God,
sing praise to our holy King;
all the earth sing praise.

He our God is King,
ruling over all nations
from His holy throne.

All the world's Leaders
assemble with the people
of Abraham's God.

Those who rule the earth
are under His dominion:
He reigns over all.

Great is the Lord God
and most worthy of all praise
in His high city.

His holy mountain,
how glorious to behold!
Joy of all the world.

Mighty Mount Zion,
the true pole of all the earth,
the great King's city!

In her citadels
God reveals Himself to be
Stronghold of the earth.

Kings march upon her;
terrified by her splendour
they flee in dismay.

Trembling had seized them.
Like a woman in labour
they writhed in anguish.

Like ships of Tarshish
threatened by easterly winds
of destructive force.

What we had been told
we now beheld for ourselves
in God's own city.

That city of His
which He, the Lord God of hosts,
upholds for ever.

We ponder, O Lord,
on Your everlasting love
within Your temple.

The praise of Your name –
from end to end of the earth –
must make itself heard.

Justice in Your hand
sets Mount Zion rejoicing
and gladdens Judah.

The peoples exult
as Your unerring judgements
put right all their wrongs.

Walk around Zion:
how many are its towers,
how strong its ramparts!

You have to pass on
to coming generations
the tale of its might.

Tell too of our God,
Who will ever be our God,
Who always leads us.

Hear this, you nations,
inhabitants of the world,
rich and poor alike.

The words that I speak
are wise, and my heart is full
of understanding.

I attune my ear
to a proverb, then expound
its truth with my harp.

In times of evil
why should I fear the malice
of treacherous men?

Of men whose whole trust
is in riches, and who boast
only of their wealth?

It is not for men
to ransom themselves from God,
to buy their release.

Nor can man purchase
an eternity of life,
thus avoiding death.

Both wise and foolish
will come at last to their grave,
stripped of all they owned.

Though their names live on,
in the grave will they remain
for all time to come.

49

Humans, like cattle,
have but a brief span of life;
their days are cut short.

This is true of fools
and true too of followers
who seek to please them.

They all rush headlong
to ever-attendant death,
just like mindless sheep.

Death is their shepherd,
herding them to the pastures
where the just hold sway.

Stripped of all honours,
their bodies will waste away
in deepest Sheol.

God will ransom me,
plucking my soul from Sheol
with His outstretched arms.

Do not, then, envy
him who sees his wealth increase.
It goes not with him!

No wealth, no glory
will follow him to the grave,
where joys turn to dust.

His prosperity,
in that pit of misery,
not even a dream.

His place forever
will be with his forefathers
in deepest darkness.

By love of riches
man forfeits intelligence
and dies like a beast.

Yahweh, God of gods,
summons the world to Himself
from east to far west.

It is from Zion,
the perfection of beauty,
that the Lord shines forth.

50

Our God is coming,
no longer wrapping Himself
in kingly silence.

A consuming fire
goes before Him; about Him
a raging tempest.

The heavens and earth
are summoned as witnesses
to His judgement seat.

"Gather before Me
all those who by sacrifice
sealed My covenant."

The heavens proclaim
the justice of His judgement,
for He, God, is Judge.

"Listen, My people;
I bear witness against you.
I am God, your Judge.

"I do not find fault
with sacrifices of yours
ever before Me.

"Nor am I claiming
an extra bull from your sheds
or goat from your pens.

"Mine, all forest beasts,
Mine, the cattle on the hills,
all teeming life, Mine.

If I were hungry,
would I turn to you for help?
Everything is Mine!

Do you imagine
that I eat the flesh of bulls,
or drink he-goats blood?

No, let thanksgiving
be your sacrifice to God;
pay your vows to Him.

In time of trouble
call on Me; and honour Me
Who come to your help.

But to the wicked
God will ask, "What right have you
to mouth my decrees?

"You who spurn My law
and scatter My commandments
to the passing winds.

"You make friends with thieves
and even throw in your lot
with adulterers.

"Your speech is evil
and you make use of your tongue
to slander others.

"Even your brother,
the son of your own mother,
suffers from your tongue.

"All these things you do
and, thinking I am like you,
count on My silence.

You who forget God
I shall tear into pieces;
no one will save you.

One who offers Me
a thanksgiving sacrifice
does Me due honour

and to such a one
I shall show God's salvation
for following Me.

51

Be gracious to me
for Your true love's sake, O God.
Blot out my misdeeds.

Wash away my guilt,
purify me from my sins,
from every offence.

I am well aware
that many are the misdeeds
preying on my mind.

Against You alone
are the evils I have done.
I have displeased You.

It is with justice
that You pass sentence on me
who am blameworthy.

I was born guilty,
a sinner from the moment
of my conception.

Through this mystery
You, Lover of faithfulness,
teach me true wisdom.

Purify my heart,
making it whiter than snow;
then shall I be clean.

Awaken me, Lord,
to rejoicing and gladness;
heal my sinful heart.

Turn Your face away
from the evils of my past;
blot out all my guilt.

Create for me, Lord,
a heart that is new and clean,
a steadfast spirit.

Never drive me forth,
from Your Presence; Your Spirit
never take from me.

Reawaken me
to the joy of true freedom
and zealous service,

so that I may lead
transgressors back to Your ways,
bring them home to You.

O God, rescue me,
and my tongue shall ever sing
of Your great goodness.

Open my lips, Lord,
and my mouth shall for ever
tell of Your greatness.

You take no delight
in our sacrifices, Lord;
You seek not our gifts.

Offerings from me
are useless; Your one desire,
my contrite spirit.

My broken spirit
is, indeed, what I bring You,
with a chastened heart.

Be favourable
to Zion, Lord, renewing
her prosperity.

May the city walls,
the walls of Jerusalem,
again be built up.

Then will You delight
in lawful sacrifices
and burnt offerings.

Again will young bulls
be offered on Your altar
as You commanded.

Why, man of evil,
do you boast all the day long
of your wicked deeds,

infamous designs
against God's loyal servant?
You plot destruction,

master of deceit,
using your razor-sharp tongue
to slanderous ends.

Lover of evil
(no place in your heart for good)
living by lying.

God will cast you down;
He will drag you from your tent
and into your grave.

Good men will look on,
awestruck at first, then laughing
at the sinner's plight.

"So much," they will say,
"for the man who would not take
God as his stronghold!

"He put his trust in
the vastness of his riches,
drew strength from his crimes!"

But I, for my part,
am like a strong olive-tree
in the house of God.

I have put my trust
in God's faithful love for me
which will know no end.

Unceasingly, Lord,
for all You have done for me
I will render thanks.

I will glorify
Your name among Your servants
and all who love You.

The impious fool
says in the depths of his heart,
"God does not exist!"

How corrupt men's hearts,
how vile and loathsome they are!
Not a good man left.

God looks from heaven
to see it any are wise,
if any seek Him.

All are unfaithful,
all are rotten to the core;
all good men are gone!

Steeped in ignorance
are those doers of evil
who hate my people.

They devour them
as though they were eating bread;
never call on God.

How scared they will be,
stricken by mortal terror,
when God rejects them.

God scatters the bones
of wicked and shameless men
who earn rejection.

If your salvation
came, Israel, from Zion,
Jacob would rejoice;

Be glad, Israel,
when God sets His people free
from chains of bondage.

By Your name, O God,
show Your power and save me,
and see justice done.

Listen to my plea:
free me from my assailants,
from these men of blood.

54

Those violent men
who wickedly seek my life
with no thought for God.

God is my support;
I know I can count on Him
to uphold my life.

May their own malice
recoil on those who hate me,
whom You can destroy.

I, with willing heart,
offer You a sacrifice
in praise of Your name.

You have rescued me
from trouble and overthrown
all my enemies.

O God, hear my prayer,
do not hide Yourself from me
as I plead for help.

Listen to my prayer
for I am beset by cares
and can find no rest.

The shouts of my foes
and screaming of angry men
cause me to tremble.

Dread is upon me.
My heart is torn with anguish,
like the pangs of death.

In fear and trembling,
and overwhelmed by horror
I await the worst.

I yearn to have wings,
to fly away and find rest
in some safe refuge.

Could I but escape
into a place of hiding
in the wilderness!

There would I shelter,
hidden away from tempests
and from raging storms,

from envenomed tongues
and the blasts of calumny
aimed at my downfall.

55

For in the city
there is naught but violence
by day and by night.

Pain and misery
stalk the public squares and streets;
sin is everywhere.

An enemy's work?
A rival's? That I could bear.
Behind this – a friend!

My own companion!
One to whom I gave my heart,
our friendship valued.

In close harmony
we strolled as one in God's house
in happy converse.

Now may death strike them!
Wickedness was in their homes
and deep in their hearts.

I shall call on God,
lamenting from morn to night,
and He will save me.

He will give me peace.
Though many foes surround me
He will hear my voice.

The eternal Judge
humbles men who honour not
their solemn pledges.

Fearing not their God
such men turn in violence
on lovers of peace.

They take oaths lightly
and, their words smoother than oil,
think only of war.

With drawn sword in hand
and words softer than butter
they are poised to strike.

Commit your fortune
to the Lord Who sustains you,
Who guards all your ways.

Them He will cast down
to the pit of destruction,
fruit of their treason.

Their days are numbered.
For my part, O Lord and God,
my trust is in You.

O God, be gracious
for one harried on all sides,
trampled underfoot.

Many are the foes
who day by day beset me,
seeking to harm me.

56

From the depths of fear
I call on You to help me.
My trust is in You.

Trusting in Your help,
I cast aside all my fear
for what men can do.

Though their words may wound
as they plan to bring me down
and seek to kill me;

though they dog my steps
and lie in wait to harm me,
You still hold them fast.

Pay back their malice.
You Who overthrow nations,
attend to my plea.

My grief has moved You;
with love You have recorded
my abundant tears.

Of this I am sure:
my foes, when I call on You,
will be put to flight.

The promise of God,
the source of my deepest trust,
and my proudest boast.

My trust is in God;
how can I possibly fear
wiles of mortal men?

I have bound myself
by vows made to You, my God;
for this I praise You.

You saved me from death,
so I walk in Your presence
in the light of life.

Be kind to me, Lord.
I, making You my refuge,
hide beneath Your wings.

I shall take shelter
under their protective shade
until storms pass by.

57

I shall call to God –
the Most High God – that in me
His will be fulfilled.

May He, from heaven,
look down in loving kindness,
keeping me from harm.

Lions surround me,
their teeth like spears and arrows,
their tongues sharpened swords.

Be exalted, Lord,
and, high above the heavens,
shine over the earth.

May those be ensnared
who, seeking to entrap me,
ever lie in wait.

Let the hidden pit,
dug to bring about my fall,
swallow up my foes.

My heart is steadfast
and my tongue will never cease
singing Your praises.

Awake, O my soul,
awake, my harp and lyre –
greet the dawn with praise.

Among the peoples
and among all the nations
I shall praise the Lord.

High as the heavens
is Your faithfulness, Lord God,
Your love without end.

Be exalted, Lord,
high above the firmament
and to the earth's bounds!

You who rule the world,
are all your decisions just?
Is fairness your aim?

No! Your hearts are hard:
your minds fixed on oppression
you sow violence.

From their mother's womb
the wicked have gone astray,
taking wrong turnings.

Poison their weapon,
they are as deaf as adders
to the charmer's spell.

Break their teeth, O Lord,
and pluck out the deadly fangs
of these savage beasts.

Let them drain away
like water running to waste,
no more to be seen.

Stricken by arrows
may they, like stillborn babies,
be denied daylight;

rooted from the ground,
as by a maddened reaper
clearing harmful thorns.

All men of virtue,
seeing vengeance has been done
will join in saying,

58

"So there is indeed
reward for the righteous.
God is a just Judge!"

O God, rescue me!
Save me, my Tower of Strength,
from my attackers.

From evil doers,
men of blood lying in wait,
rescue me, O God.

For no sin of mine,
for no wilful transgression,
they seek to harm me.

Rise up, Lord; help me!
God of hosts, Israel's God,
be my Defender.

Punish the nations,
and have no mercy on those
who are treacherous.

At nightfall they come,
slavering like maddened dogs
prowling through the streets.

They roam here and there
and snarl if not satisfied
in their search for food.

Abuse streams from them,
wounding words spew from their lips
when they are ignored.

But You, Lord, mock them,
You Who deride great nations,
You Who give me strength.

59

God, my Strong Tower
will ever go before me
in unfailing Love.

I shall, with God's help,
gloat over those who mocked me,
who sought to harm me.

Will You not kill them
lest people come to forget
the wrongs they have wrought?

May Your mighty arm
scatter them, Lord, to the winds,
bring them to ruin.

By their own words, Lord,
let them come to destruction,
entrapped by their pride.

Let them be cut off
for their cursing and their lies,
consumed by Your wrath.

Then will God be hailed,
known as Ruler in Jacob
to earth's farthest ends!

They roam here and there
and snarl if not satisfied
in their search for food.

For my part, great Lord,
I will celebrate Your strength
at the break of day.

It is You, O Lord,
Who have been my Citadel,
sure Help in trouble.

To You, Lord, this psalm,
You Who are my Strong Tower,
my surest Defence.

60

You have cast us off,
You, O God, have broken us,
used us cruelly.

Come back to us, Lord.
The earth is trembling, quaking,
has been torn apart.

You have made us drink
bitter draughts of suffering,
a wine that dazed us.

Yet You had forewarned
those who served and feared You,
letting them escape.

Come and deliver
all who count on Your friendship.
Save and answer them.

From His holy place
God has made us this promise:
"With exultation

"I Who have triumphed
will now divide up Shechem
parcelling it out.

"I will moreover
divide the Succoth Valley
into plots of land.

"Gilead is Mine;
Mine also is Mannasseh,
Ephraim My helm;

"Judah is My staff.
Moab will be My washbowl,
Edom My vassal.

"Who now will cry out
'Victory!', Philistia,
target of My wrath?"

But who will lead me
to overthrow the fortress,
to vanquish Edom?

Will You reject us,
no longer lead the armies
with which You marched, Lord?

Help us in this hour
for the help of man is vain,
utterly useless.

With You on our side
we shall fight valiantly, Lord,
and tread down our foes.

61

Hear my cry for help;
listen, Lord, to my pleading,
my shout of distress.

From far off places
my plea is coming to You,
though my heart is faint.

Set me up on high,
on a rock beyond my reach,
You, my sure Refuge.

Let me stay with You,
under cover of Your wings
hidden in Your tent.

You, God, hear my prayer,
and grant me the heritage
of those who fear You.

May the king live on,
his years prolonged for ever,
enthroned in Your sight.

May he be guarded
by Your Love and Faithfulness
to the end of time.

Your Name I shall praise
in fulfilment of my vows
as long as I live.

My soul in silence
is awaiting God alone –
Him, my Salvation.

He alone my Rock,
my Fortress, my Salvation.
I shall not be moved!

62

How long do you need
to bring down a helpless man
weakened by your blows?

You plan his defeat.
While your lips utter blessings
in your hearts you curse.

My soul rests in God,
waits for the deliverance
He alone can grant.

He is my Fortress,
my mighty Rock, my Stronghold,
my one sure Shelter.

Trust Him, you people
on whom He bestows His love.
He is our Refuge.

Man: a puff of wind;
mighty men: a delusion;
lighter than the air!

Count not on power,
put not your trust in treasures
nor your heart on gold.

Once has God spoken,
twice has it been repeated:
all power is His!

Love, too, is Yours, Lord,
and You will make us payment
as our works deserve.

God, You are my God;
my heart eagerly seeks You,
my soul thirsts for You.

Parched is my body
like a long-unwatered land
as I await You.

My eyes are straining
to see Your glory light up
the Sanctuary.

Your unfailing love
is better than life itself;
my lips will praise You.

So will I bless You:
my voice raised in Your honour
throughout all my days.

My soul satisfied
as by the richest of feasts,
I will sing your praise.

Lying on my bed
on You I muse through the night
recalling Your help.

I know I am safe
in the shadow of Your wings,
and I sing for joy.

My soul clings to You
as Your right hand holds me fast,
ever my strong Shield.

63

May all who seek me,
those planning my destruction,
go down to the depths.

Condemned to the sword,
may they be left as the prey
of starving jackals.

The king will rejoice
in the God by Whom he swears,
all falsehood silenced.

Hear, O God, my plea,
and grant me Your protection
from threats of my foes.

Conceal me, my God,
from doers of evil deeds
and their wicked plots.

64

They sharpen their tongues
as though they were two-edged swords;
their words like arrows.

From ambush they shoot
suddenly and recklessly
at the innocent.

Everything is planned
and they confidently ask,
"Who, then, will see us?"

He Who searches minds,
Who knows the depths of the heart
will overthrow them.

With His own arrow
God, without any warning,
will shoot and wound them.

Them He will destroy,
use their own words against them,
terrifying them.

Then will all men fear;
they will tell what God has done
and understand why.

Just men will rejoice
and fly to God for refuge,
giving Him glory.

To God in Zion
we render dutiful praise,
paying Him our vows.

You, O God, hear us
as, with our burden of sin,
we come before You.

65

Too heavy for us
are our many offences,
but You blot them out.

Blessed is the one
whom You choose and call to dwell
in Your holy courts.

May we find pleasure
in the blessings of Your house,
Your holy temple.

Your righteousness,
God of our deliverance,
richly repays us.

The ends of the earth
and all far-distant islands
put their hope in You.

You uphold mountains,
with Your strength set them in place;
Your might surrounds them.

You calm the clamour
of tumultuous oceans,
bring peace to peoples.

nations in uproar
at the sight of Your wonders
are filled with great joy.

You care for the earth,
make it fruitful in Your sight,
multiply its yield.

You crown with goodness
the abundance of the gifts
that mark Your footsteps.

What was wilderness
has become by Your passing
gentle pastureland.

Hills are bright with joy,
meadows are covered with flocks,
valleys dance with wheat.

Shouts of joy ring out,
voices raised in happiness,
sounds of joyful song.

Earth, acclaim your God,
glorify His holy name,
shout aloud His praise.

Delight in saying,
"How tremendous are Your deeds!
How great Your power!"

66

Foes cringe before You,
overcome by Your great strength.
The whole world bows low,

singing in Your praise:
"Come and see what God has done,
how awesome His deeds!

"People crossed the seas
He had turned into dry land,
crossed rivers on foot."

We rejoice in Him
Who rules by power and might,
Whose eyes miss nothing.

Let no rebels rise
in defiance of their God.
May they bless His name.

May high praise resound
to the honour of our God
Who gives life to souls!

You have tested us
and kept our feet from stumbling,
tried us like silver.

Even into snares
have You, God of might, led us,
heavily burdened.

You have allowed men
to ride rough-shod over us;
yes, over our heads.

But now our ordeal
has come at last to an end
and we can draw breath.

So I bring to You
holocausts in fulfilment
of the vows I made:

my burnt offerings
of bullocks and fatling goats
and of burning rams.

All you who fear God,
listen while I acknowledge
His goodness to me.

Had my thoughts been black
the Lord would not have listened –
but He did listen.

Blessed be the Lord
Who did not reject my plea,
nor withhold His love!

O God, be gracious;
let Your face shed upon us
Your radiant smile.

Then will Your purpose
and Your saving power be known
to every nation.

67

May all the nations
and all the people on earth
know and praise You, Lord.

May they sing with joy
at the thought of Your justice
ruling over them.

Let all the nations
loudly sing Your praise, O God,
their hearts full of joy.

Earth yields its harvest
for You, once again, O God,
have poured gifts on us.

May our God bless us,
that, to the ends of the earth,
His name be revered.

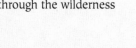

68

When God arises
His enemies will scatter,
all His foes will flee.

As smoke in a draught,
as wax too close to a flame,
so with the wicked.

But with God's approach
the just will exult and sing,
cry aloud with joy.

O sing to the Lord
as, riding upon the clouds,
He comes among you.

Father of orphans,
Defender of the widowed,
God in His heaven!

God from His heaven
sees the lonely, and gives them
a home of their own.

He leads prisoners
forth to freedom and safety –
not so the rebels.

They remain enchained;
there they must dwell forever
in an arid land.

As You went forth, Lord,
at the head of Your people
through the wilderness

the earth rocked and quaked.
As You marched through the desert;
heaven poured down rains.

You lavished riches
upon Your starving people,
giving them new life.

They built themselves homes
in the land You provided;
You cared for their needs.

The Lord gives the news
to bearers of good tidings:
"Our foes are scattered!

"Kings and armies flee;
women were heaping up loot
while you were at rest!"

Like the wings of doves
they are covered with silver,
bright with shining gold.

Snow on Dark Mountains –
even so did jewels glint
on Bashan's high peaks.

A mountain of God!
He has placed His own dwelling
on those lofty heights.

Could human eyes gaze
upon peaks chosen by God
for His dwelling place?

Beyond numbering
are the divine chariots
surrounding the Lord.

To the holy place
has the Lord come from Sinai
with all His captives.

You receive, O Lord,
all that is brought in tribute –
even the rebels!

Blessed be the Lord,
He Who bears, day after day,
all of our burdens.

He, a God Who saves,
Keeper of the keys of death
Who strikes down His foes.

He has no mercy
on those who parade their guilt,
who persist in sin.

The Lord has promised:
"From Bashan I will bring them,
even from the depths.

"Paddling in their blood,
you will summon your war dogs
to share in the feast."

Now, Lord, is our gaze
fixed upon Your procession,
a kingly progress,

as it makes its way
towards the sanctuary,
led by Your cantors.

Then come musicians
amongst whom there are maidens
playing tambourines.

Bless God in your choirs;
you who spring from Israel,
loudly sing His praise.

There is Benjamin
at the head – least of the tribes;
then, Judah's princes.

Zebulon's princes,
the princes of Naphtali.
God, show forth Your might.

Take command, O God,
befitting the great power
You wield for our sake.

Demand of kings, Lord,
from the heights of Your Temple
the tribute they owe.

Threaten the wild beast,
the herds of bulls, all people
dwelling in the reeds.

Make them bow down low,
offering silver and gold;
crush those warmongers.

Envoys from Egypt,
Nubian ambassadors,
must bow before You.

Kingdoms of the earth,
sing loudly your praise to God
Who rides the heavens.

Listen to His cry,
give ear to His thundering,
acknowledge His might.

Great is the glory
of the God of Israel,
ever to be feared.

He, Israel's God,
gives power to His people.
Blessed be our God.

146

Save me, O my God,
for the waters are rising,
are up to my neck!

I am sinking deep
into the mud of the swamp;
there is no foothold.

69

Swept out of my depth,
I am carried by the flood
into wild waters.

My throat is rasping
because of all my shouting,
and my sight is dimmed.

I await Your help.
People, far beyond counting,
hate me without cause.

Attacked by their lies
I have been robbed of my strength
and cannot face them.

How can I restore
what I have never stolen?
You, Lord, know the truth.

You know my follies;
naught is hidden from Your sight.
Blame none for my deeds.

Let those who trust You
not be shamed on my account,
Yahweh Sabaoth.

May none who seek You
suffer humiliation
because of me, Lord.

For Your sake, O Lord,
I suffer taunts and insults,
in shame hide my face.

I, to my brothers,
have become an alien,
a stranger to them.

I am eaten up
with zeal for Your holy house;
insults rain on me.

When I fast in tears
my foes make it a pretext
for insulting me.

If I wear sackcloth.
I become their laughing stock,
taunted as a fool.

At the city gates
people gossip about me
and sing drunken songs.

I for my part, Lord,
continue to pray to You
as in days of old.

In Your great love, God,
grant me sure deliverance,
save me from the mire.

Pluck me from this swamp;
do not allow me to sink.
Free me from my foes.

Drag me from the depths
before I am swept away
into the abyss.

In loving kindness,
turn to me, Lord, and answer.
Pay heed to my woes.

Draw close to my soul
and bless me with redemption
from my foes' assaults.

Taunts and derision
shower down upon my head;
my heart is broken.

Overwhelmed by grief,
I seek for understanding
but find no support.

When thirst assails me
they offer me vinegar;
for hunger, poison!

May they be ensnared,
enticed by their own banquets
to ghastly ruin.

Let their eyes grow dim
until darkness surrounds them,
may ague shake their limbs.

Pour out upon them
Your indignation, O Lord;
their homes leave empty.

Their tents abandoned
because they persecuted
one whom You struck down,

because they increased
the pains You had in justice
seen right to inflict.

Charge them with their crimes
and close to them all access
to righteousness.

May their names, Lord God,
be blotted out forever
from the Book of Life,

struck off forever
from rolls wherein are inscribed
names of the godly.

As for me, O Lord,
wretched sinner though I be,
raise me up on high.

I will praise God's name,
extol Him with thanksgiving,
singing His glory.

A gift pleasing God
more than sacrificial beasts
are my songs of praise.

Joy fills humble hearts,
those who seek Him are revived;
He spurns not the poor.

Friend of the enchained,
heaven and earth, sea and fish –
forever praise Him.

God will save Zion
and rebuild Judah's cities
as homes for His friends.

Then will their children
have a rich inheritance.
All will bless God's name.

Show me Your favour
and come quickly to my help.
Rescue me, O God.

Let shame and disgrace
fall on those who are seeking
to do me to death.

Confuse and shame, Lord,
those who delight in my ills,
who jeer at my lot.

May all who seek You
be filled with joy and gladness,
crying, "God is great!"

Come quickly to me,
poor wretch that I am, O Lord,
make haste to save me.

70

I have found in You
the refuge I seek, O Lord.
Let me not be shamed.

By Your saving grace
rescue and deliver me,
hear me and save me.

71

Rock of my refuge
wherein I can find shelter
and lasting safety!

For You are my Rock.
a walled fortress to save me
from rogues and tyrants.

In You alone, Lord,
trusted from my youngest days,
can I place my hope.

From my very birth
I have leaned upon You, Lord;
even from the womb.

A portent to some,
an enigma to many,
my trust is in You.

You are my refuge,
my mouth is full of Your praise,
hymning Your splendour.

Now that I am old
and my strength is fast failing,
do not reject me;

I am under threat
from the foes who surround me
and hatch wicked plots:

"Hound him!" is their cry,
"for God has deserted him;
he is in our hands!

"Take fast hold of him
for there are none to help him!"
Do not fail me, Lord.

May shame and ruin
fall on those who attack me;
may they be disgraced!

My heart full of hope,
I shall go on praising You
ever more and more.

My lips will loudly
proclaim Your righteousness,
Your power to save.

The Lord's mighty deeds
I shall declare; His justice
the theme of my praise.

As day follows day
I shall never cease telling
of Yahweh's great deeds.

Not yet must I die,
since rising generations
must hear of God's might.

To all must I speak
praising Your strength and justice,
proclaiming Your might.

Who, Lord, is like You?
You burdened me with troubles
but gave back my life.

You will raise me up
from depths deep beneath the earth
to joy in old age.

Your great faithfulness,
theme of my praise with the lute,
ever faithful God.

I will sing You psalms
accompanied by the harp,
God of Israel.

My heart filled with joy,
I will thank You on the harp
for my redeemed soul.

All day long my tongue
shall tell of Your just dealings,
O righteous One!

May shame and disgrace
fall upon the heads of those
who seek to harm me.

With Your justice, Lord,
robe the King; and to His Son
give righteousness.

Thereby will he rule
Your people with good judgement
and Your poor justly.

The mountains and hills
will bring forth peace and justice
for all the people.

May the King defend
the poor among his people,
those in sorest need.

Children of the poor
he must save from oppression,
crush their oppressors.

His reign shall endure
like sun and moon, without end
for age upon age.

Like a gentle rain
that falls upon growing crops,
so is His blessing.

To the righteous
He will bring prosperity
and lasting justice.

May He long hold sway:
His empire from sea to sea,
His bounds to earth's end.

His foes will bend low
and displaced kings will hasten
to pay Him tribute.

Sheba and Seba,
dispossessed of their kingship,
will bring Him rich gifts.

Kings will pay homage,
their subjects bow before Him –
all now His servants.

The poor He will feed.
All who call upon His name
will be given help.

The poor and the weak
will count upon His kindness
and He will save them.

He will liberate
all victims of extortion,
all the exploited.

To Him they are dear.
(They will never cease blessing
His benefactions.)

Plentiful the grain
in every part of the land,
to the mountain tops!

May crops continue
to flourish like Lebanon:
like grass on the earth.

May His name be blessed,
for ever may it endure
as the sun endures!

May all the peoples,
every race throughout the world
ever bless His name.

Blessed be Yahweh,
mighty God of Israel,
Who alone is great.

Blessed for ever
be all His wonderful works,
His glorious name.

Amen and Amen.
May His glory fill the earth.
Amen and Amen.

God is good indeed
to His people Israel,
to all of pure heart.

Yet I was stumbling.
My feet slipping under me,
and I almost fell.

I was envying
the proud who amass great wealth
by their evil deeds.

They, it seemed to me,
are always healthy and strong,
suffering no pain.

Unlike most people
they appear to be spared
human affliction.

Their chain of honour
is the pride they love to flaunt
by violent deeds.

Malice fills their hearts,
their minds seethe with villany
and deceitful plots.

Cynical mockers,
advocates of oppression,
they sneer at goodness.

They look on themselves
as heavenly oracles –
with malicious tongues.

73

People turn to them;
and, believing what they hear,
cast doubt on God's word.

They begin to ask,
"Does the Lord know everything?
Does He even care?"

Such are the wicked!
See how untroubled they are –
and how their wealth grows!

Was it all in vain
that I kept my hands from guilt,
my heart unsullied?

As day follows day
I am beset by torment,
suffer affliction.

By speaking like that
I would be a traitor to
the race of Your sons.

Then must I wrestle
with a problem which I find
beyond my powers.

I must seek to probe
the ways of the Almighty
when faced with evil.

It then dawned on me
that the lives of wicked men
are slippery slopes.

There You have them stand
heedless of what awaits them.
Suddenly they fall!

Their terror kills them.
You dismiss them as phantoms,
a frightening dream.

My embittered mind,
failing to fathom Your plans,
had been resentful.

So, cut to the quick,
I became a brutish beast,
unworthy of You.

Yet I was with You,
You had hold of my right hand
to give me courage.

Never leave me, Lord.
Be my Guide and Counsellor.
Lead me to glory.

Whom have I but You?
And having You, my Lord God,
what else can I need?

Though my heart fail me,
and my body find no peace,
You, forever mine!

For those far from You
there is only destruction
and ultimate doom.

With You is my joy.
I have chosen You, O Lord,
as my sure Refuge.

Is it for ever
that You, Lord, have cast us off?
Why are You angry?

We are Your flock, Lord,
the sheep You used to pasture,
the tribe You redeemed.

You chose Mount Zion
as Your favoured dwelling-place
where You loved to rest.

Tread now these ruins,
weep in the sanctuary
stripped of its altars.

The shouts of Your foes
re-echoed through the Temple
beneath their banners.

Their foreign emblems
are profaning the entry
to the Holy Place.

Doors have been battered
with their mallets and hatchets,
devoured by flames.

They are profaning
and mean to raze to the ground
the house where You dwelt.

They are determined
to destroy us for ever,
to hack down our shrines.

74

No sign from our God,
no prophet left to tell us
how long this will last.

For how long, O Lord,
will these enemies taunt us,
and treat You with scorn?

Why do You wait, Lord,
and keep Your right hand hidden
within Your bosom?

O King from of old!
Protector of all the land,
grant us timely help.

By Your own power
You crushed Leviathan's heads
and fed them to sharks.

For springs and torrents
You ripped open wide channels
and dried up rivers.

Days and nights are Yours,
the light and the shining sun
appointed by You.

It was You who fixed
the earth's bounds and created
summer and winter.

Recall now, Yahweh,
the blasphemy of Your foes,
how they insult You.

Israel, Your dove,
give not over to the hawk.
Betray not Your poor!

Your Covenant, Lord,
must be upheld for ever;
we can bear no more.

Violence prevails:
every cave in the country
is under attack.

Leave not the oppressed
in the hands of wicked men
for they too praise You.

Never close Your ears
to the clamour of Your foes
nor forget their crimes.

We give You thanks, Lord,
and, calling upon Your name,
we recount Your deeds.

We are drawing close
to the time when true justice
will begin to reign.

Then, when the earth rocks,
I will dispense strict justice
on all who dwell there.

I poised its columns
so to the boastful I say,
"Do not praise yourselves!"

And to the wicked:
"Do not flaunt your strength on high
nor speak so boldly!"

Not from east or west,
nor from deserts or mountains
shall judgement come forth.

God Himself is Judge:
one man He will bring down low
another raise up.

The Lord holds a cup.
full of spiced and foaming wine –
but heavily drugged.

When He pours it out
all the wicked of the earth
must drink to the dregs.

Never will I cease
singing loudly the praises
of Israel's God.

Wicked men He breaks;
but He further empowers
all righteous men.

Great is Judah's God,
renowned through all Israel,
in Salem His tent.

He dwelt in Zion
where he broke flashing arrows,
shields, swords and armour.

You, Illustrious!
Resplendent and Majestic!
How great is Your name.

Despoiled warriors
are sleeping the sleep of death,
for their arms failed them.

At a word from You
horses with their chariots
were cast to the ground.

You, the Terrible!
Who can oppose Your onslaught
or face Your anger?

When You, from heaven,
made known to men Your sentence
all were struck silent.

You arose to judge:
and by that judgement You saved
those in greatest need.

The wrath of the proud
by increasing Your glory
gives joy to Your friends.

Make vows to Your God
and offer Him the tribute
due to His power.

He curbs the spirit
of the princes of the earth,
leaving them awestruck.

When I raised my voice,
calling loudly on my God,
He deigned to listen.

In my deep distress
I raised my hands to the Lord
by day and by night.

Unceasing my tears
for I could not be consoled,
refused all comfort.

Remembering God,
I gave way to groans and sighs;
my spirit failed me.

You robbed me of sleep,
made me too distraught to speak
of days that had passed

Throughout the long night
I tossed about in distress,
sank into despair.

Will God reject us?
Will He never more show us
His love and favour?

Is the Lord's promise
rendered void for evermore?
His mercy withheld?

"My deepest distress
comes," I said, "from the knowledge
that God's ways have changed."

I recalled the past,
the achievements of Yahweh,
the marvels of old.

I mused on His works,
pondering His mighty deeds ...
and remained perplexed.

God's ways are holy.
What god is great as our God,
He Who works wonders?

Nations have witnessed,
have been forced to acknowledge
the might of Your hand.

With Your own right arm
You have redeemed Your people,
the Patriarch's sons.

The very waters,
at the sight of You, O Lord,
recoiled and drew back.

At a word from You
thunderous clouds poured down rain
while the lightning flashed.

Thunder crashed and rolled,
Your lightning lit up the world,
all the earth shuddered.

You strode through the sea,
wading through mighty waters
Your footprints unseen.

The Guide of Your flock,
You led Moses and Aaron
to their journey's end.

Pay heed, My people,
to the words I am speaking
and take them to heart.

By means of stories
I will disclose to Your minds
secrets of the past.

The things we have heard,
which we came to understand,
things passed down to us

must not be hidden
from coming generations;
they must be passed on.

All our descendants
will need to urge their children
to trust in God's love.

All must remember
what He did for His people;
all must keep His Law.

They must not become,
like many of their forbears,
men of fickle heart.

Sons of Ephraim,
those skilful and famed bowmen,
turned tail in battle.

Spurning God's commands
and forgetful of His might
they threw off His Law.

78

Their fathers had seen
the marvels performed by God
on Egyptian soil.

There He struck the sea
and they, through walls of water,
marched along dry shod.

During daylight hours
a cloud led them; at night time
a fiery glow.

He gave them water
that gushed forth from solid rocks
in endless torrents.

In that wilderness
they still angered the Most High,
still disobeyed Him.

They challenged their God,
ordering Him to serve them
with delicacies.

In blasphemous terms
He was urged to supply them
with a festive meal.

"He did," they jested,
"give us water – but not bread!
And where is our meat?"

When He heard these words.
Yahweh's anger was aroused
against His people

Angered by Jacob,
furious with Israel
for their lack of trust

He, nevertheless,
still ordered the skies above
to rain down manna.

Heaven's vaults opened
and let fall around their tents
the bread of angels.

Food in abundance
was there to be gathered up –
more than they could eat.

Winds from east and south
conjured up by Yahweh's might
rained down food like dust.

While they were eating
God's anger rose against them
laying many low.

The strongest were slain,
those young men of Israel
were brought to the ground.

Yet still that people
persisted in their sinning,
put no trust in God.

He ended their days
in emptiness and ruin;
then did they seek Him!

He, they remembered,
was their Rock and Redeemer
their Deliverer.

But the words they spoke
were nothing but flattery
and mere lip-service.

In His compassion
He forgave them and spared them
again and again.

He never forgot
they were mere creatures of flesh,
passing puffs of wind.

In that wilderness
they frequently defied Him,
causing Him sorrow.

Again and again
they put their God to the test,
blind to His mercy.

He had redeemed them
from their Egyptian masters
by means of ten plagues.

Rivers turned to blood,
waters from which none could drink,
vast swarms of horseflies.

Frogs molested them,
locusts ruined their harvests,
grubs fed on their crops.

Hail broke down their vines,
sycamores succumbed to frost,
flocks to pestilence.

The heat of His rage
was turned on their oppressors,
fury and havoc.

The angels of death
strode among them, striking down
all their first-born males.

His people, like sheep,
He led through the wilderness,
safe and unafraid.

And as they escaped
their enemies were engulfed
by the raging sea.

And so He brought them
to the frontiers conquered
by His own right hand,

driving out nations
and settling His people
in their new dwellings.

Yet still those people
went on challenging their God,
mocking His decrees.

They soon proved themselves
as faithless as their fathers,
warped and useless bows.

They angered the Lord
with their shrines to pagan gods
and carved images.

So enraged was God
He rejected Israel
and forsook Shiloh.

No more would He dwell
in the tent He had chosen
among His people.

He consigned His ark
into the hands of His foes:
to captivity!

His own dear people
He surrendered to the sword,
so great was His wrath.

Youg men to the flames,
brides weeping and lamenting
in their widowhood.

Then the Lord awoke
like a man aroused from sleep
or maddened by wine.

He struck down His foes,
attacking them from behind
until all had fled.

The clan of Joseph
and the tribe of Ephraim
He struck from His plans.

Judah was His choice,
the sanctuary He loved,
built on Mount Zion.

His servant David
He brought forth from the sheepfold
from the care of ewes

to the pasturing
of the people of Jacob,
His dear Israel.

With a blameless heart
and singleness of purpose
David led God's flock.

79

The pagans, O Lord,
invading Your heritage,
profaned Your Temple

and Jerusalem
they have reduced to ruins.
Your servants' bodies

have been cast as food
to the birds of the heavens,
Your friends to the beasts.

Jerusalem's streets
are all awash with their blood,
as though with water.

Our dead unburied,
we suffer our neighbours' taunts,
derided by all.

How much longer, Lord,
will Your anger against us
smoulder like a fire?

Address Your anger
to the nations that hate You,
that dismiss Your name,

to those who reduced
all the dwellings of Jacob
to desolation.

You must not blame us
for all the crimes committed
by our ancestors.

Out of love for us
intervene on our behalf
or we shall be crushed.

O God, our Saviour,
for the honour of Your name
blot out all our sins.

Why should the pagans
feel free to mock us, asking
"Where then is their God?"

Let them be repaid
for all the blood they have shed
of men dear to You!

May the captives' groans
reach You and win them reprieve
from the threat of death.

Seven times over
may the insults of Your foes
be repaid by You.

And may Your people,
the flock of Your pasturing,
ever praise Your name.

Listen to our cry,
O Shepherd of Israel,
shine forth from Your throne.

You Who lead Joseph,
as a shepherd leads his flock,
come now to our help.

Shine on Ephraim,
Benjamin and Manaseh
and rouse up Your might.

Come to restore us.
Save us, Yahweh Sabaoth,
and we shall be safe.

Lord, how much longer
will You go on resisting
Your people's pleading?

Sorrow is our food,
and tears in abundance
all we have to drink.

Our neighbours mock us,
enemies laugh us to scorn ...
God, come to our help.

Smile on us again,
rescue us and keep us safe,
Yahweh Sabaoth.

From Egyptian soil
You uprooted a strong vine
ready for planting.

80

You drove out nations,
cleared a space for it to grow
and watched it take root.

It filled the country,
its shade covered the mountains
like massive cedars.

It spread wide its boughs,
stretched out its shoots to the sea,
to the great river.

The walls now destroyed,
You have allowed passers-by
to eat of its fruit.

The boars ravage it
wild animals tear at it.
Come, Yahweh, save it.

Look down from heaven
at this vine You had planted
and which men have burnt.

The frown of Your face
will bring about the ruin
of those despoilers.

Grant that Your right hand
will ever rest on the man
whom You have chosen.

Endowed with Your strength,
no more shall we abandon
the Giver of life.

Grant us now new life
that we may call on Your name,
Yahweh Sabaoth.

Bring us back to You
and let Your face shine on us
that we may be saved!

Let us shout for joy
in honour of God our strength,
the God of Jacob!

Sound pipe and tabor,
the sweet-sounding harp and lute,
voices raised in song.

Herald the new moon;
make music for the full moon
on this great feastday.

The God of Jacob
has imposed on Israel
this solemn statute.

So was it decreed
when Joseph went forth to fight
the men of Egypt.

A mighty voice cried,
"I freed you from your burdens,
relieved your distress.

"Thunder spoke My words,
Meribah's streams tested you.
Now you must hear Me:

"Turn from foreign gods.
I Who led you from Egypt
am your Lord and God.

"I am impatient
to satisfy all the needs
you make known to Me.

"My people failed Me,
Israel would not obey,
heeded not My words.

"I abandoned them
to their stubbornness of heart,
to their own designs.

"Would that Israel
was ready to heed My voice,
would walk in My ways!

"With one single blow
I would strike down all their foes,
all who attack them.

"The Lord's enemies
would cringe at His people's feet,
suing for mercy.

"Then would I feed you
with finest wheat and honey
to your hearts' content."

Yahweh takes His place
in the divine assembly
to dispense justice.

"Injustice must end;
the poor and the dispossessed
must be judged fairly.

"Orphans and the weak
must be snatched from the clutches
of rapacious men.

"Greedy and heartless,
such men are undermining
the earth's foundations.

"I said, 'You are gods,'
yet even the Most High's sons
die like other men.

"Just as princes fall,
so has it to be with you."
O God, judge the earth,

pass on Your justice
to the nations of the world,
since You rule them all."

83

Be not silent, God.
Be neither quiet nor still
at Your foes' outcry.

See how proud they are,
how arrogantly they stand
plotting evil schemes.

They are weaving plots
against those whom You protect,
against Your people.

"Down with them!" they cry;
"we shall wipe from memories
Israel's proud name!"

They plot together –
Edomites, Ishmaelites,
Moab and Hagar,

Gebal and Ammon,
Amalek, Philistia
and the Tyrians;

Assur has joined them,
reinforcements for Lot's sons.
They must be treated

as was Midian,
as Sisera and Jabin
suffered at Kishon.

Like those of En-dor
where the bodies of the slain
rotted on the ground.

Treat their generals
just like Oreb and Zeeb
and their commanders;

as once you treated,
both Zebah and Zalmanna
who had proudly sworn

to take possession
of the Dwelling of our God.
Scatter them, O Lord,

like chaff before wind,
like tumbleweed in a gale,
like flames through forests.

Drive them before You
like fire leaping on mountains,
caught in a whirlwind.

Cover them with shame
till they seek safety with You
and honour Your name.

May they learn at last
that You alone are the Lord,
High above all earth.

How dearly loved, Lord,
is the place where You reside,
the Court of heaven.

How happy are those
Lord of hosts, my King and God,
who dwell in Your house!

84

Sparrows find a home,
the swallows a nesting place
close to Your altar.

O Lord God of hosts,
happy those who dwell with You,
their praise unending.

Joyful the pilgrims
who have been sent forth by You
on their pilgrim way.

The bitter Valley
they see as a place of springs
blessed by autumn rains.

Thence, from height to height
they go, all their hopes set on
the God of Zion.

Look kindly on us
and bless with many favours
Your anointed one.

One day in Your courts
surpasses thousands of days
spent anywhere else.

The steps of God's house
a more delightful dwelling
than a sinner's home.

God our Battlement,
Giver of grace and glory
our Shield and Armour,

He will not refuse
to those who walk without blame
any of His gifts.

O Lord God of Hosts,
happy indeed are Your friends
whose trust is in You!

85

How graciously, Lord,
have you revived the fortunes
of the land You love.

Your people who sinned
are granted deliverance,
Your anger allayed.

Bring us back, O Lord
when we seek deliverance
through Your saving help.

Are You still angry?
Is Your wrath everlasting,
prolonged forever?

Give us life again
granting cause for rejoicing
with Your love and help.

I am listening
to what Yahweh is saying
for His words bring peace.

Peace for His people
whom, their folly forgiven,
He counts as His friends.

His help is at hand
for those whose hearts worship Him;
glory enfolds them.

Love and faith have met,
justice and peace have embraced:
heaven sees – and smiles.

Now shall we prosper
through the goodness of the Lord;
our earth shall bear fruit.

His justice leading
and peace following His steps
we march at His side.

86

Listen to me, Lord,
and answer my plea for help
in my wretchedness.

Save me, Your servant
who is constant and faithful,
who relies on You.

Show Your favour, Lord;
I call to You all day long,
awaiting Your help.

Grant that Your servant
find reason for rejoicing
and lightness of heart.

Kind and forgiving,
You overflow with love, Lord,
when we call on You.

Listen to me, Lord.
Knowing how wretched I am
heed my cry for help.

None among the gods
is to be compared with You,
nor their deeds with Yours.

The pagan nations
will come to bow before You
and honour Your name.

For You are mighty,
wonderful are all Your works,
Who alone are God.

Show me, Lord, Your way,
that I may walk in Your truth,
O Guide of my heart.

I shall praise You, Lord,
with an undivided heart
acclaiming Your name.

Great Your love for me,
whom You have deigned to rescue
from Sheol's dark depths.

Now I am attacked
by brutal and ruthless men
who give You no thought.

But You, Lord, are God,
compassionate and gracious;
turn and pity me.

Protect Your servant;
save the son of Your slave-girl
as proof of Your love.

Put my foes to shame
at the sight of Your goodness,
my help and comfort.

God in His great love
founded on the holy hills
His chosen city.

To Him Zion's gates
are dearer and more cherished
than Jacob's dwellings.

There He makes His home,
delighting in the glory
He finds within them.

Egypt, Babylon
He has placed among His friends,
as those who know Him.

Philistia, Tyre,
Ethiopia are there,
counted as His own.

Zion, named "Mother,"
gives welcome to all nations,
calls all "my children."

The most High Himself,
He writes in His register,
"These are her children."

And, dancing, they sing,
"In You, all will find their home,
source of every good."

To You, Lord my God,
I call for help day by day;
I weep all night long.

Let my prayer reach You,
hear the cries of deep distress
pouring from my soul.

My soul is troubled,
the grave, as though I were dead,
seeks to engulf me.

I am accounted
as one already buried,
tossed beside the slain.

Remembered no more,
I am cut off from Your care
in these tomb-like depths.

Your wrath weighs me down
since You have brought Your fury
to bear upon me.

I cannot escape;
my eyes are veiled with anguish,
dimmed by suffering.

Day after day, Lord,
I have called to You in prayer,
stretching out my hands.

Will, then, Your wonders
be kept for those who are dead?
Will the shades praise You?

Will they, from the grave
tell of Your love and sure help
in that place of doom?

Will Your wondrous deeds
be told in those dark regions,
Your greatness lauded?

But for my part, Lord,
I ceaselessly call for help,
morning, noon and night.

Why am I cast off?
Why are You hiding Your face,
rejecting my pleas?

From my early days
death has been lying in wait,
terror has numbed me.

Perils surround me,
ever closing in on me.
All my friends have gone.

Yes, friends and neighbours,
all have been wrested from me.
Bitter the darkness!

Of Your loving deeds
I shall sing forever, Lord;
praise them to the sky.

Through all the ages
my mouth will proclaim Your truth,
fixed as the heavens.

89

"With My chosen one
I have made a covenant,
pledged word to David.

"Your line shall endure,
your throne remain established
to endless ages."

The heavens, O Lord,
proclaim Your wonderful works,
the angels Your truth.

In the skies above
who can compare with Yahweh,
who can rival Him?

A God to be feared
in the heavenly council,
terrible His might.

O Lord God of Hosts,
clothed in strength and faithfulness,
there is none like You.

You rule the wild sea,
calm the turmoil of its waves
and still its thunder.

The monstrous Rahab
You crushed with a single blow,
then scattered Your foes.

The heavens are Yours,
Yours the earth and its wonders,
the works of Your hand.

You founded the world
and everything it contains –
from north unto south.

Tabor and Hermon
cry out with joy at Your name,
praising Your great strength.

Your hand is mighty;
Your right arm high uplifted
tells of Your power.

Justice and good faith –
are the pillars of Your throne,
love and truth Your seal.

Happy the people
who have learnt to acclaim You,
on whom Your face shines.

Always and ever
they exult in Your goodness,
the source of their bliss.

You are their glory.
Thanks to Your strength and favour
we hold our heads high.

The Lord is our shield.
Holy One of Israel,
You are our Ruler.

We recall the time
when, in a vision, You told
Your friends the prophets:

"I have set the crown
on the head of a hero
whom I have chosen.

"My servant David,
selected and anointed
king of My people.

"Upheld by My hand,
strong with the strength of My arm,
him shall none outwit.

"No wicked person
shall become his oppressor
nor stand over him.

"His foes I shall crush
and, his opponents silenced,
smite all who hate him.

"Wherever he goes,
he will be accompanied
by My loving trust.

"And he, through My name,
will ever hold his head high,
his rule established.

"To Me he will say,
'You are my Father, my Rock
where I find safety.'

"He shall be to Me
My firstborn, highest among
the kings of the earth.

"There will be no end
to the love I have for him,
to our sworn friendship.

"I will establish
his dynasty for ever,
an unending line.

"If his sons fail Me,
flouting My law and judgement,
deaf to My commands,

"them shall I punish
with the rod and with lashes,
though still loving them.

"My love will remain.
My sworn promise to David
I will not renounce.

"His posterity
shall never come to an end,
his throne like the sun.

"As sure as the moon,
it will endure forever,
a faithful witness."

Yet have You not spurned,
rejected the holy one,
whom You anointed?

Have You not broken
Your covenant with David,
his crown dishonoured?

You have broken down
the walls of his fortresses,
laid them in ruins.

Now he is plundered
by all who are passing by
while his neighbours mock.

You have let his foes
flaunt their power over him
with unbridled joy.

His great sword blunted,
You left him to fight alone,
his glory obscured.

His throne in the dust,
You have brought to a sad end
his youth and promise.

How much longer, Lord,
will You hide Yourself from sight
Your wrath unrestrained?

Remember, O Lord,
how short the span of our lives
and their emptiness.

Can man cling to life,
dismissing the claims of death
and Sheol's powers?

What has become, Lord,
of Your mercies of the past
promised to David?

Do not forget, Lord,
that Your servant is taunted,
mocked by the people.

Your enemies, Lord,
continue to rail at us
wherever we go.

Blessed be the Lord.
    Amen and Amen!

From age to age, Lord,
we have always looked on You
as our sure refuge.

Long before mountains
and the earth and world were born
You alone are God.

You give the command
and men revert to the dust
from which You formed them.

A thousand year span
seems to You a passing day,
a watch in the night.

You brush men away
like a dream at break of day
or withering grass.

It springs up at dawn,
flowers during daylight hours,
then fades and dries up.

So are we destroyed,
brought to nothing by Your wrath,
victims of our fears.

You behold our guilt,
our sins open to Your gaze,
our secrets revealed.

Our days pass away,
the years drift by silently,
like a sigh are gone.

Our span seventy
or possibly eighty years
for those who are strong.

At best, years of toil,
often bearers of sorrow;
then, soon, we are gone.

The strength of Your wrath –
only those who honour You
have felt its full force.

Reveal to us, Lord,
the brevity of our life,
and grant us wisdom.

Show us Your mercy.
Satisfy us with Your love
at the break of day.

We shall sing for joy;
spending our days in gladness
and casting off grief.

May Your saving grace
be granted to Your servants
and to their children.

May the Lord's favour
surround us and give success
to all that we do.

If you live under
the shelter of the Most High,
dwelling in His shade

you can say to Him,
"You, my Refuge, my Fortress,
are the One I trust!"

He will rescue you
from the snare of the fowler
and deadly danger.

He will cover you,
His pinions a shield for you
when danger threatens.

His truth your buckler,
you will have no need to fear
the terrors of night,

nor arrows by day;
nor pestilential darkness
and plagues at noonday.

Thousands of victims
may be stricken around you,
you will not be touched.

Your own eyes will see
the downfall of the wicked.
But you, who can say

"God is my refuge,"
have a secure dwelling-place,
free from disaster.

For you, He commands
His angels to be on watch
wherever you go,

to spring to your aid
should there be any danger
of your falling down.

On snake and serpent,
asp and cobra you will tread
and remain unharmed.

"Because he loves Me,
and holds fast to My commands
I shall protect him.

"Since he knows My name,
I shall answer when he calls
in time of trouble.

"I shall rescue him,
honour him and content him
with fullness of days."

What a joy it is
to render thanks to the Lord,
to sing Yahweh's praise!

To greet the morning
by acclaiming His great love
and, at night, His truth.

All to the music
of the zither and lyre
and a ten-stringed harp.

I am made happy
by the greatness of Your deeds.
They fill me with joy.

How wonderful, Lord,
are all Your undertakings,
how profound Your thoughts!

Foolish men are blind
to the wonder of such works,
far beyond their grasp.

Such men sprout like weeds
while evil-doers prosper –
but all shall perish.

You, Lord, are supreme;
Your reign shall last forever
while they fall to dust.

You raise high my head
like the horns of wild oxen,
anoint it with oil.

I gaze in triumph
on the ones You have brought low,
those who hated me.

Now will good men thrive
and stand tall like the cedars
on Lebanon's heights.

Planted in Your house,
flourishing within Your courts,
their fruit is assured.

Sturdy in old age,
vigorous and full of sap,
those wide-spreading trees

bear lasting witness
to the just and faithful Lord
till time is no more.

Yahweh is our King
robed in majesty and might,
girded with power.

The world You made firm
and Your throne unshakeable
before time began.

93

The waters, O Lord,
lift up their thunderous voice,
hurl their monstrous waves –

yet, mightier still
than roaring, crashing waters
is the Lord Most High.

Your decrees stand firm,
holiness befits Your house
throughout the ages.

94

Lord, God of vengeance,
show Yourself, avenging God!
Rise, Judge of the earth.

Strike the arrogant,
give the wicked their deserts.
They must not triumph!

How long will they boast
about their evildoing,
puffed up with conceit?

They crush Your people,
oppress Your chosen nation,
prey upon the weak.

Widows and strangers
and the fatherless children
are their chief victims.

"The Lord does not see,"
they laugh; "the God of Jacob
pays no heed to them!"

Watch out for yourselves,
fools, most stupid of people!
Learn while there is time.

He Who made the ear,
does He not Himself listen?
The Maker of eyes

is He Himself blind?
The Instructor of nations
never points out faults?

Was mankind's Teacher
likely to deprive Himself
of needful knowledge?

The Lord is aware
that the thoughts of everyone
are less than a breath.

Happy is the one
to whom the Lord grants knowledge
of His holy law.

Such a one is safe
from misfortunes that await
lovers of evil.

The Lord will never
forsake His chosen nation
and those who trust Him.

Justice will triumph
and this the upright of heart
will at once embrace.

Who will stand by me,
defend me from the wicked?
Who is my Defence?

Without the Lord's help
I would soon have been buried
in the silent grave.

When my foot had slipped,
Your sustaining love, O Lord,
kept tight hold of me.

When doubts assailed me
and filled my heart with sadness,
You brought me comfort.

How could the corrupt
count You, Lord, as their ally
in base lawlessness?

Those who plan murder,
the death of the innocent,
of the righteous!

God is my Stronghold.
He has ever been for me
my Rock and Refuge.

He will wreak vengeance
on lovers of injustice,
give them their deserts.

Praise the Lord with joy,
acclaiming Him Who saves us,
Rock of our safety.

Let us approach Him
with our songs of thanksgiving,
singing His triumphs.

95

Almighty the Lord,
a great King above all gods,
the world in His hand.

The depths of the earth
and the peaks of the mountains
all belong to Him.

Seas, works of His hand,
and the dry land which He shaped
were all made by Him.

Let us, then, enter
and bend low in deep homage
to Him Who made us.

For He is our God,
we the people He shepherds,
the flock in His care.

Listen to His voice;
you will come to understand
how great is His might.

"Harden not your hearts
as you did at Meribah
and once at Massah.

"There in the desert
your forefathers challenged Me
then saw for themselves.

"For forty long years
their complaining wearied Me
until I cried out,

"'Their hearts are astray;
they cannot discern My ways,
nor My plans for them.'

"Then, in My anger,
I swore that not one of them
would enter My rest."

O sing a new song;
sing to Yahweh, all the earth,
a song that is new.

Sing and bless the name
of Yahweh, our Most High God;
proclaim His kindness.

96

Declare His glory,
make it known to the nations,
to all the peoples.

How great is the Lord!
How worthy of the world's praise!
Greatly to be feared.

Heathens' gods are naught,
whereas He Whom we adore
made heaven and earth.

Majesty and might
are in His sanctuary;
splendour and beauty

shine in all His deeds.
Pay Him tribute, you peoples!
Give Him due esteem!

Honour Yahweh's name,
bring offerings to His court.
Tremble before Him.

Cry to the nations
"Yahweh, earth's Maker, is King,
true Judge of the world!

Rejoice, you heavens!
Earth and seas, shout in gladness!
May the fields exult

and all that they bear,
with the trees of the forests,
shout aloud their joy

before Him Who comes,
the Lord, Ruler of the earth.
He will judge the world

and all its peoples
in His justice and fairness,
faithfulness and truth.

Yahweh is our King;
let the earth and its coastlands
rejoice and be glad.

He is surrounded
by clouds and misty darkness;
His throne, truth and right.

97

Fire precedes Him
consuming foes on all sides;
lightning fills the skies.

Earth sees and trembles
as great mountains melt like wax
at the Lord's approach.

The heavens proclaim
the Lord of righteousness;
all see His glory.

Servers of idols
and lovers of images
shrink away in shame.

Bow down, heathen gods.
The Lord of heaven and earth
passes before you!

Zion, triumphant,
heard Your judgements and rejoiced
with Judah's cities.

For You, Most High Lord,
are Ruler of all the earth,
far above all gods.

Beloved by the Lord
are all who hate wicked ways.
With Him they are safe.

These, His faithful friends,
He rescues from the clutches
of their enemies.

Light dawns for the just,
joy for the upright of heart.
Give praise to His name.

With new songs of praise
let us render due homage
to the Lord's great deeds.

He has worked wonders;
His right arm and holy hand
have wrought miracles.

98

His the victory.
All the nations bear witness
to His saving might.

Never forgotten
that love He bears for Jacob
and his descendants.

The ends of the earth
have seen our God's victory
and have acclaimed it.

Now let all the earth
acclaim Him with songs of joy,
honour Him with psalms.

To music of harps
and instruments of all kinds
we shall praise His name.

To trumpet and lute
and sound of echoing horn
acclaim Yahweh King!

Let the sea thunder
and all that lives within it;
may all the rivers

clap their hands for joy
while the mountains lift their heads
at Yahweh's presence.

For He comes to us
as Judge of earth and peoples
in justice and truth.

He will judge the world
according to strict justice,
always in fairness.

Yahweh is our King,
throned upon the cherubim;
nations are trembling.

The earth is quaking
at the greatness of the Lord
enthroned on Zion.

99

High above nations,
His holy name is extolled
by all the peoples.

Holy, powerful,
a King Who loves what is right,
judging with justice.

You have established
honesty and equity
as once for Jacob.

Exalt our Lord God,
bowing before His footstool,
for He is holy.

Moses and Aaron
were numbered among His priests,
They, like Samuel,

called upon His name.
When they called upon the Lord,
He answered their prayers.

He conversed with them
beneath a pillar of cloud.
They kept His decrees,

obeyed the statutes
which He, the Lord, had given
for their observance.

You, O Lord our God,
answered them and forgave them;
Yet You called on them

to give an account
for all of their wrongdoing.
Exalt our Lord God

bow down before Him.
Revere His holy mountain,
for He is Yahweh.

Cry out to Yahweh,
all you peoples of the earth;
sing praise to His name.

Joyously praise Him
as you enter His presence
singing your gladness.

Acknowledge that He
is our mighty Lord Yahweh
and we His people.

He created us,
the flock of His pasturing;
we belong to Him.

Enter then His gates,
filling His court with the sound
of our thanksgiving.

How good is the Lord!
How great His merciful love
and His faithfulness!

Kindness and justice,
these are the themes of the psalm
I sing to Yahweh.

I move towards You
on the way to holiness.
Will You come to me?

Within my household
I seek to live blamelessly,
keeping my heart pure.

My eyes never stray
nor conjure up sordid deeds
and disloyalty.

I hate crooked ways,
apostasy repels me,
evil I disdain.

Men of perverse hearts
I try to keep at arm's length,
as I do sinners.

Secret slanderers
I swiftly bring to silence.
The proud I banish.

I choose as my friends
the most faithful in the land;
servants whom I trust.

Treacherous persons
will find no place in my house;
nor will hypocrites.

Men who utter lies
shall not stand before my face
nor win my favour.

Morning by morning
I seek to drive from our land
all who do evil.

For there is no place
in the city of the Lord
for evildoers.

102

Hear, Yahweh, my plea;
let my cry for help reach You.
Do not hide Your face.

In my sore distress
be attentive to my needs;
answer me quickly.

My days pass away.
They are vanishing like smoke,
my bones smouldering.

My heart, like scorched grass,
is fast shrivelling away;
I can hardly eat.

Loud is my groaning
for, nothing but skin and bone,
I have lost my strength.

Lost in the desert,
like an owl among ruins,
alone on a roof.

Throughout the long day
my foes, mocking and taunting,
conspire against me.

My bread is ashes,
tears fall into my goblet,
so great is Your wrath.

He Who raised me up,
now in furious anger
flings me to the ground.

As shadows lengthen
so are my days declining
like withering grass.

You, Lord, are enthroned,
Your name assured for ever –
famed from age to age.

Rise and take pity.
Have mercy, Lord, on Zion.
Now is mercy's hour!

The appointed time,
the time for mercy, has come;
take pity on her.

Every stone of her
is beloved of Your servants.
They are moved to tears

even by her dust.
Nations shall fear the Lord's name,
kings proclaim His fame

when Zion rises
and, in a display of might,
He comforts the weak.

This will be set down
for future generations
who too will praise Him.

For the Lord leaned down
from His high sanctuary
to survey the earth.

Groans of prisoners
reach Him, moving Him to free
those condemned to die.

So shall the Lord's name
be highly praised in Zion
and Jerusalem

whenever people
are assembled together
in the Lord's service.

My strength is waning
before my course has been run.
Little time is left.

"Do not snatch me off
before half my days have gone!"
I entreat the Lord.

Long, long ago, Lord
You laid the earth's foundations
and made the heavens.

All else will vanish
like clothes that have been cast off,
moth-eaten garments.

But You will remain,
the unchanging Creator,
Your years without end.

[Your servant's children
will be, with their descendants,
set in Your presence.]

Bless the Lord, my soul.
I, from the depths of my heart,
bless His holy name.

Bless the Lord, my soul,
and forget not the blessings
He pours out on me.

He forgives my guilt,
pardons me my wrongdoings
and heals all my ills.

He redeemed my life
when His love and compassion
plucked me from the grave.

He satisfies me
with good things; renews my youth
like that of eagles.

Righteous His deeds,
He is just in His treatment
of all the oppressed.

With Moses He shared
what He planned to do to help
the Israelites.

The Lord is gracious,
full of compassionate love,
patient and faithful.

He does not find fault,
never nurses resentment,
is quick to forgive.

103

He does not treat us
in accordance with our sins,
knowing our weakness.

As high as heaven,
towering above the earth,
so is the Lord's love

for those who fear Him.
As far as east is from west
He casts all our sins.

Just as a father
takes pity on his children,
the Lord pities us.

For He is aware
of everything about us;
knows that we are dust.

Our days are like grass:
we blossom like wild flowers,
are felled by a breath.

A mere gust of wind
and there is no longer proof
we once existed.

From those who fear Him
the Lord will not withdraw love,
nor from His children.

He will never fail
those who keep His covenant
and honour His Law.

The throne of the Lord
is established in heaven
with worldwide power.

Angels, bless the Lord,
give thanks, you mighty host
who obey His word.

Give thanks to the Lord,
ministers who do His will,
armies who serve Him.

All created things,
bless the Lord's wide dominions.
My soul, bless the Lord!

104

Bless the Lord, my soul!
Lord my God, how great You are,
clothed in majesty!

Enfolded in light,
You have spread out the heavens
like a festal tent.

Your palace You build
upon heavenly waters,
clouds Your chariots.

As You ride the wind
You make it Your messenger,
and flames Your servants.

The earth You have fixed
firmly on its foundations,
never to be moved.

The deep covered it
as with a cloak, while waters
stood high as mountains.

At Your word, they fled,
at the sound of Your thunder
dashed madly away,

flowing over hills,
pouring down into valleys,
their allotted place.

Boundaries You fixed
beyond which they must not pass
to cover the earth.

You made springs gush forth
in valleys and between hills
where wild beasts might drink.

Nesting on their banks
were many birds of the air
singing joyful songs.

From Your dwelling-place
You water hills and valleys,
enriching the earth.

You make pasturage
for the cattle, plants for men
to sustain their strength.

Bread springs from the earth,
and wine to gladden our hearts,
oil to comfort them.

Trees You make flourish:
tall cedars of Lebanon
where birds build their homes

and storks nest on high.
Hills, the haunts of mountain goats,
rocks where badgers hide.

The moon is Your work,
marker of months and seasons;
the sun tells the hours.

Your darkness brings night;
while beasts prowl in the forest
young cubs growl for prey.

When the sun rises
they slink away to their lairs,
seeking rest and sleep.

Man goes forth to work,
labouring throughout the day
till evening falls.

Countless Your works, Lord!
The products of Your wisdom,
all made by Your hand.

The sea, vast and wide,
with creatures beyond number
restlessly swimming.

Ships sail to and fro
while the great Leviathan
there disports himself.

All depend on You
to supply the food they need
as day follows day.

Whatever You give
they gather up eagerly,
thus to eat their fill.

When You hide Your face
they are fearful and dismayed
as hunger threatens.

When You take their breath
they die and return to dust
from whence they were made.

When You breathe again,
new beings are created,
fresh life for the earth.

May Your glory, Lord,
ever fill the earth with joy
in all that You do.

You look, the earth quakes.
When You touch the mountaintops,
smoke pours forth from them.

Throughout all my days
I shall be praising the Lord,
ever singing psalms.

May my prayerful thoughts,
as I delight in His love,
be pleasing to Him.

May sinners vanish
from the face of the Lord's earth,
to be seen no more!

Bless the Lord, my soul
Give praise to the Lord!

105

Give thanks to the Lord,
invoking His holy name,
making known His deeds.

Call on Him with song,
praise His name with holy psalms,
recount all His deeds.

Exult in His name
and may all those who seek Him
be joyful in heart.

Look then to the Lord,
you offspring of Abraham,
recalling His strength.

Children of Jacob,
His chosen ones, remember
the marvels He wrought.

He, the Lord, is God.
His authority on earth
must always prevail.

God, with Abraham,
made a solemn covenant,
with Isaac, an oath.

He declared and swore,
"This land is your heritage,
Canaan now is yours!"

While few in number,
a mere handful of strangers,
they were wanderers.

Hither and thither
they went, but God was with them,
and none oppressed them.

He admonished kings
who dared to hinder their plans,
"Do My friends no harm."

He called down famine
and cut off their daily bread,
but watched over them.

He sent before them
Joseph, sold by his brothers
into slavery.

His feet were fettered,
iron encircled his neck
in a prison cell.

He foretold events
that were soon to come to pass;
the king set him free.

He made him master
within the royal household,
handler of his wealth.

Teacher of princes,
instructor of the elders –
all was in his hands.

Thus did Israel
make its way into Egypt,
and Jacob dwelt there.

Made fruitful by God,
the people soon outnumbered
those who envied them.

The hearts of their foes
were overcome by hatred;
they planned their downfall.

Moses, God's servant,
and Aaron His chosen one
sent as His envoys

brought God's messages,
with mighty signs and portents
to the land of Ham.

First He sent darkness –
the whole land wrapped in darkness –
but to no effect.

Waters became blood
and all the fish therein died;
frogs covered the land,

even the king's court.
Then there came swarms of dogflies
and, after them, gnats.

God sent storms of hail;
then terrifying lightning
ruined all their crops.

Their vines and their trees
were shattered throughout the land.
Then, swarms of locusts!

Finally, first-born
of humans and beasts alike
were struck down by death.

God's people marched forth
laden with silver and gold,
not one left behind.

The whole of Egypt
rejoiced to see them leaving,
so great was their fear.

By day they were screened
as by great masses of clouds;
at night, led by flames.

When hunger threatened,
flocks of quail fell around them,
bread rained on their camp.

In that barren land
streams of life-giving water
flowed forth from a rock.

For God remembered
the promise He had made to
faithful Abraham.

He led His people
towards that land of promise,
rejoicing with them.

He granted to them
vast pagan territories
which became their own.

on one condition:
that they observe His statutes
and obey His laws.

Give thanks to the Lord
for His goodness, and His love
which lasts for ever.

How can we praise Him,
our God Whose wonderful deeds
are far beyond words?

106

Happiness is ours
when we always act justly
and do what is right.

Remember me, Lord,
out of the love that You have
for all Your people.

Be my true Saviour
that I may share the glory
of Your chosen ones,

rejoicing with them
in our nation's great gladness
and exultation.

Like our forefathers
we have given way to sin,
we have gone astray.

They, when in Egypt,
paid no heed to God's marvels,
forgot His great love.

They, at the Red Sea,
raised their voices against Him,
yet did He save them.

He delivered them
for the sake of His own name,
to make known His might.

At the Lord's command
His people walked through the sea
as though on dry land.

Thus did He save them
from the hands of oppressors,
the grip of their foes.

Then the wild waters
closed over their pursuers
leaving none alive.

His people praised Him
and were ready to believe
all He had promised.

But soon they forgot
the things He had done for them,
deaf to His counsel.

Insatiable greed
gripped them in the wilderness,
trying God's patience.

He yielded to them
but sent disease among them,
a wasting sickness.

They were envious
of Moses and his brother,
whom God had chosen.

The earth opened up
and it swallowed up Dathan
with Abiram's clan.

Fire raged among them
and the rebel company
perished in the flames.

They fashioned a calf
out of metal at Horeb
and bowed before it.

They exchanged their God
for the image of a bull,
a beast that eats grass.

They forgot their God,
He Who had done such great things
to liberate them:

marvels in Egypt,
awesome deeds at the Red Sea.
He would destroy them!

Moses stood by them.
The man whom God had chosen
turned back His anger.

Still they had no faith
in what the Lord had promised,
scorned the plans He made.

They muttered treason
when they gathered in their tents,
and would not obey.

With uplifted hand
He swore an oath to slay them
in the wilderness;

all their descendants
He would scatter through the lands,
among the nations.

They bowed down before
the Baal of Peor, and ate
sacrificial meals.

God's wrath was provoked
and upon them fell a plague,
which Phinehas checked.

His intervention
has counted in his favour
throughout the ages.

Then at Meribah
God's wrath was again aroused
by their complaining.

The Lord was angered
when the people's murmuring
so enraged Moses

that he spoke rashly,
then afterwards regretted
the things he had said.

They failed to destroy
according to God's command,
tribes that displeased Him.

They made pacts with them,
paid homage to their idols
and followed their ways.

Their sons and daughters
they began to sacrifice
to false deities.

The innocent blood
of their children they poured out
to honour false gods!

They defiled themselves
by such deeds and broke their bond
with the Lord Most High.

His anger blazed out
in loathing for His people,
His chosen nation.

Those who hated them
He allowed to master them,
to tyrannise them.

Yet time and again
He returned to rescue them.
Still they defied Him.

When He heard their cries
He, recalling His promise,
pitied their distress,

and, with boundless love,
aroused in their captors' hearts
feelings of pity.

Deliver us, Lord;
from among all the nations.
Bring us together,

that we may give thanks
to Your ever holy name,
praising Your glory.

Blessed be the Lord,
the one God of Israel,
now and forever.

Amen! Amen! Alleluia!

Give thanks to the Lord!
His love is everlasting.
How good to thank Him!

Let all the redeemed,
saved by Him from enemies,
join in thanking Him.

All those He gathered
out of lands from east to west
and from north to south.

Some strayed through deserts
seeking a place to dwell in,
but they searched in vain.

Hungry and thirsty,
their spirit faint within them,
they called on the Lord.

He heeded their cry
and led them from their distress
to welcoming towns.

Let them give Him thanks
for the wonder of His love
for all humankind.

He quenches their thirst,
fills the hungry with good things,
consoles the enchained.

Some sat in darkness,
bound fast with iron fetters
for defying God,

107

for flouting His Law
and spurning the commandments
of the Most High Lord.

Their spirit subdued
by their long imprisonment
they had lost all hope.

They in their troubles
called on the Lord's Holy Name
and He rescued them.

He sundered their chains
and brought them forth from darkness
to the light of day.

Thanks be to the Lord
for the wonder of His love
for all humankind.

He has battered down
gates made of bronze, and shattered
sturdy iron bars.

Some had been foolish,
adopting rebellious ways
and so were punished.

Sickened by their food,
some were at the gates of death
and called on the Lord.

Hearing their pleading
He sent His word to heal them
and snatch them from death.

Let them give Him thanks
for the wonder of His love
for all humankind.

They, with joyful cries,
must offer sacrifices
in whole-hearted praise.

Others sailed the seas,
plying their trade as merchants
on the wide waters.

They saw for themselves
the mighty deeds of the Lord
in those vast oceans.

With only a word
He raised up terrible gales
lifting high the waves.

Ships were tossed sky-high,
then plunged down into the depths,
crews like drunken men.

Their skills failing them
they called to the Lord for help,
and all became calm.

Amidst rejoicing
they were led to the haven
they had been seeking.

Let them then thank God
for His never-failing love
and wonderful works.

Let all give Him praise
as they gather together
in the assembly.

He transforms rivers
into deserts at one word,
springs into dry ground.

Land which once bore fruit
He now, because of their sins,
turns into salt flats.

Deserts become pools,
parched lands become at His word
springs of fresh water.

The hungry have homes,
sites for building up townships,
land for growing crops.

Fields for their sowing,
for the planting of vineyards
to bear rich harvests.

He pours out blessings
which ensure increase for them
and for their livestock.

Tyrants lose their strength.
They fall into misfortune,
oppression and grief.

He pours His contempt
on princes of noble birth,
now become vagrants.

The poor He raises
high above their former plight
and gives them increase.

The upright see this
and rejoicing brims over
while the wicked mourn.

Whoever is wise,
let him, in gladness of heart,
ponder on God's love.

My heart is steadfast.
O God, my heart is steadfast.
I shall sing Your praise.

Awake, then, my soul;
Awake, O harp and lyre,
and herald the dawn.

Among the peoples
I, O Lord, shall praise Your name
and lift up a psalm

among the nations
for Your faithfulnes and love
to heavenly heights.

Be exalted, God,
above the highest heavens
and may Your glory

encompass the earth.
With Your strong right hand
free those whom You love.

From His holy place
God has promised to divide
the land of Shechem.

The vale of Succoth
He will also make over
to one He chooses.

Gilead is mine
as is also Manasseh;
Ephraim My helm,

108

My sceptre Judah;
Moab I use as washbowl,
Edom my footstool;

My war cry I hurl
triumphantly at the men
of Philistia.

But who will show Me
the impregnable city,
guide Me to Edom?

Do you, God, intend
utterly to reject us?
to desert our ranks?

Face our foes with us!
In vain do we look for help
among mere mortals.

With Your help, O Lord,
we shall battle like heroes,
trample down our foes.

109

O God Whom I praise,
do not refuse to answer
when foes attack me.

My name is defamed
as they calumniate me,
lying to my face.

Hatred surrounds me.
I who offered them friendship
am repaid with scorn.

In return for love
they accuse me unjustly
while I pray for them.

"Find a venal judge"
they cry; "one who will find him
guilty of our charge!"

When judgement is passed
that rogue will be found guilty
and his sin exposed.

May his days be few.
let his hoarded wealth be seized
and fall to others.

Reduce his children,
orphaned and driven from home,
to utter ruin!

Let his creditors
seize all his goods, and strangers
flee with his earnings.

May all desert him
and none pity his children.
May his line die out.

May his father's sins
be recalled, his mother's shame
never forgotten!

May God keep in mind
all these things, while wiping out
his name from the earth.

No kindness in him,
he hounded the downtrodden,
driving them to death.

Lover of cursing,
may his cursing of others
now recoil on him.

Scorner of blessing,
may the blessings he now needs
not be granted him!

He took to cursing
like one donning a garment;
let him chafe in it!

May it wrap him round
like the clothing he puts on,
like a tight girdle.

May Yahweh repay
like this all my detractors,
all who speak evil.

You, O Lord, my God,
deal with me as befits You;
act in my defence.

Deliver me, Lord,
in the goodness of Your love;
be my rescuer.

Poor and downtrodden,
my heart within me distraught,
I call on Your help.

My life is fading
like an evening shadow,
a brushed off locust.

Made weak by hunger,
my flesh is wasting away,
I am thin and gaunt.

What have I become?
An object of public scorn,
a mere laughing-stock.

Help me, Lord my God!
Save me in Your great mercy
and abiding love.

Let all men know, Lord,
that You alone have done this
as proof of Your love.

They curse, but You bless.
Let my enemies be shamed
but let me rejoice.

May my accusers
be covered with dishonour,
wrapped around with shame.

My voice will be raised
in praise of the Lord Most High
in the Assembly.

He defends the poor
against those who condemn them
to undeserved death.

110

The Lord's oracle
having turned to my lord, said
"Sit at My right hand;

"I shall break your foes.
I shall make of them footstools
underneath your feet."

Yahweh will widen
the scope and sway of Your realm,
your rule in Zion.

Kingly dignity
was yours from the day of birth
on the holy heights.

Royal from the womb,
from the very earliest
moment of your life.

God has sworn an oath:
"You are a priest forever
of the priestly line

of Melchizedek."
This He will never retract.
He stands at your side.

If He is angered,
in the power of His wrath
He will shatter kings.

He will treat nations
according to their deserts,
piling corpses high.

As He passes by
He will drink from wayside streams
and hold high His head.

I shall thank the Lord
when the Assembly gathers,
give Him heartfelt thanks.

Great are the Lord's works
and well worth pondering on
by all who love them.

All He undertakes
mirrors His might, His glory,
His matchless justice.

His wonderful deeds
are as unforgettable
as His kindly love.

To those who fear Him
He gives all the food they need,
as He had promised.

Lands of the nations
He bestrowed on His people,
making known His might.

In truth and justice
He carries out all His works.
His precepts are sure.

These He established
to stand through all the ages,
in truth and justice.

The deliverance
of His people was a gift
and a covenant

which will have no end.
His name fills our hearts with awe,
awakens our dread.

The fear of the Lord:
the beginning of wisdom,
the proof of sound sense.

Praise Him forever!

112

Praise the Lord.

Happy are all those
who fear the Lord and delight
in doing His will.

All their descendants
will be powerful on earth,
ever richly blessed.

Their homes will be filled
with treasures, and their justice
never overthrown.

A light in darkness
for the upright, their dealings
merciful and fair.

Lending through pity,
their actions always honest,
nothing will shake them.

Because they trust the Lord
they, in the day of battle,
never dread defeat.

They, open-handed,
pour out gifts on the needy
who honour their name.

The wicked see this
and grind their teeth in anger,
all their hopes thwarted.

Servants of the Lord,
O, praise the name of the Lord;
pay Him your homage.

May His holy name
be blessed now and forever,
through all the ages.

From the sun's rising
even unto its setting
may His name be praised.

The Lord our great God
towers above all nations,
His throne in heaven.

Who is like Yahweh?
Our God so highly enthroned
deigns to look on us.

Seated with princes
are weak and lowly peasants
raised up from dungheaps.

Wives who were childless
He makes happy with children
and somewhere to live.

113

O praise the Lord.

When, out of Egypt,
came alien Israel,
the sons of Jacob,

then Judah became
the sanctuary of God,
His very kingdom.

At so strange a sight
the seas fled, and the Jordan
turned back on its course.

Mountains skipped like rams
while the hills danced and frolicked,
as playful as lambs.

Seas, why did you flee?
what decided you, Jordan,
to veer from your course?

And you, great mountains,
why were you skipping like rams,
you, hills, like yearlings?

Tremble and quake, earth,
at the presence of the Lord,
the God of Jacob.

He it is Who turns
rocks into pools of water,
flint into fresh springs.

Not to us, O Lord,
but to Your name give glory
for Your love and truth.

Why should the heathens
who surround us be asking,
"Where then is their God?"

115

We know that our God,
Who does whatever He wills,
is in high heaven.

Their foolish idols
are made of silver and gold
by the hands of men.

Although they have mouths
they are unable to speak;
their eyes cannot see.

Ears that cannot hear
and nostrils that cannot smell!
Their hands feel nothing,

their feet cannot walk
and not so much as a sound
comes forth from their throats.

Soon those who made them,
all who put their trust in them
will become like them.

Sons of Israel
turn trustfully to the Lord,
their help and their shield.

The house of Aaron
places its trust in the Lord,
its help and its shield.

All who fear the Lord
happily trust in the Lord,
their help and their shield.

He remembers us
and therefore will He bless us,
house of Israel.

The house of Aaron,
both high and low who fear Him,
these the Lord will bless.

The Lord grants increase
to you and all your children.
May He bless you all.

He, Maker of all;
heaven belongs to Yahweh,
earth He grants to man.

From their silent graves
the dead can no longer praise
the name of the Lord.

But we, the living,
shall bless Yahweh's holy name
now and forever.

Praise the Lord.

I love the Lord God
Who has listened to my cry
and heard my appeal.

Because He stoops down
to hear me, I shall always
turn to Him in need.

When the cords of death
and the anguish of the tomb
were surrounding me,

when anguish and fear
almost had me in their grip,
I called on His name:

"Lord, deliver me!"
Righteous and merciful,
Tenderhearted God!

The simple-hearted
can count on His loving help
when they are brought low.

Be at peace, my heart,
the Lord has delivered you,
has saved you from death.

My soul saved from death,
my eyes kept from shedding tears,
my feet from stumbling.

In the Lord's presence
in the land of the living
I shall walk again.

116

I had expected
to be swept away to death
and sore was my grief.

In panic I cried,
"No one can be relied on."
Now I must repay

the Lord for His love,
for all His goodness to me.
To Him Who saved me

I shall raise my cup
offering Him libations,
invoking Yahweh.

I shall pay my vows
in presence of the people
to Him Who saved me.

Precious in His sight
is the death of the devout.
I, Lord, am Your slave.

Yes, I am Your slave,
son of a pious mother,
whose bonds you have loosed!

To You I offer
a thanksgiving sacrifice,
invoking Your name.

Ever shall I walk
in the presence of Yahweh
among the living.

My vows to Yahweh
will be offered publicly
in full assembly,

in the Lord's own courts
in your midst, Jerusalem.
To the Lord be praise!

Nations, praise the Lord,
extol Him, all you peoples
for His watchful love.

Strong indeed His love,
eternal His faithfulness.
Blessed be Yahweh!

117

Give thanks to the Lord
for He is good, and His love
endures for ever.

Let it be proclaimed
by the house of Israel:
"His love has no end!"

All who fear the Lord
should add their voice, proclaiming:
"His love has no end!"

When, in deep distress,
I called on the Lord, He heard
and gave me relief.

With Him on my side
nothing can make me afraid;
who could cause me harm?

If He is with me,
what other help do I need
when foes attack me?

It is far better
to seek refuge with the Lord
than to trust princes.

Pagans surround me
but in the name of the Lord
I drive them away.

They swarm about me
but in the name of the Lord
I put them to flight.

118

They swarm round like bees,
attack like flames burning scrub;
with Him, crush them.

They thrust against me,
sought to bring me to the ground
but the Lord helped me.

The Lord, my refuge;
the Lord is my sure defence,
my deliverer.

From the victors' camp
shouts of triumph reach our ears.
The Lord has prevailed.

We have been raised up
by the Lord's powerful deeds,
by His strong right arm.

No, I shall not die.
I shall live to bear witness
to the Lord's great deeds.

Often has the Lord
imposed punishment on me,
but not unto death.

He opens to me
gates that lead to victory
that I may thank Him.

This is the Lord's gate,
the entrance He throws open
only to His friends.

I shall praise You, Lord,
for You have answered my plea
and delivered me.

The rejected stone,
unwanted by the builders,
is His corner-stone.

So does the Lord act.
How wonderful it appears
to our earthly eyes!

This, then, is the day
made memorable by Him.
Day of rejoicing!

Deliver us, Lord.
Liberty we ask of You,
and prosperity.

Blessings be on Him
Who enters in Yahweh's name!
Blessings from His house.

The Lord gives us light.
Branches in hand, we approach
His holy altar.

You, Lord, are my God.
I render You thankful praise
and extol Your name.

Give thanks to Yahweh
for His wonderful goodness,
His enduring love.

119

Aleph Those of blameless life
are happy in embracing
the law of the Lord.

Their doing His will
and diligent search for Him
bring them happiness,

for they do no wrong
and make it their chief concern
to obey His law.

You, Lord, have made known
the precepts to be observed
in all diligence.

I dearly desire
to be utterly faithful
to all Your statutes.

If I concentrate
on observing Your commands,
I shall not be shamed.

By learning Your law
with sincerity of heart
I shall praise Your name.

It is my one aim
to observe all Your statutes;
never forsake me.

Beth How can young people
keep themselves from sinfulness?
By obeying You.

I, with all my heart,
seek You; do not let me stray
from Your commandments.

What You have promised
I treasure within my heart,
lest I offend You.

How blest are You, Lord;
how glorious the statutes
You are teaching me.

Again and again
my lips repeat the rulings
which fell from Your mouth.

I find my pleasure in the
things you have have taught me –
joy beyond all wealth.

I muse on Your words;
my meditation keeps them
alive in my heart.

I delight in them;
those oft-repeated statutes
I shall not forget.

Ghimel   Favour Your servant:
let me live and, in living,
be true to Your word.

Open, Lord, my eyes
so that my concentration
be fixed on Your law.

Exile though I am,
hide not from my earthbound self
Your law's commandments.

My soul is consumed
with my incessant seeking
after Your decrees.

You threaten the proud:
accursed are those who turn back
from Your commandments.

From scorn and contempt
may I ever remain free,
who respect Your laws.

Though earthly powers
scheme and plot to bring me low,
Your statutes shield me.

My greatest delight
has its roots in Your teachings,
my sole counsellors.

Daleth   I, prone in the dust,
call on You to revive me
with life-saving words.

My fault acknowledged,
You answered and restored me;
teach me Your statutes.

Make me understand
the way of Your commandments;
I would muse thereon.

In my misery
I am unable to rest.
Renew my strength, Lord.

Guard me from falsehood;
grant me the grace of always
living by Your law.

I have made my choice:
my eyes fixed on Your decrees
I shall walk in truth.

I cling to Your law
in the knowledge that You, Lord,
will never fail me.

I will run the course
set before me by Your laws
to gladden my heart.

He   Expound to me, Lord,
the way of Your commandments,
and how to keep them.

Give me readiness
to observe wholeheartedly
whatever You teach.

Guide me in the path
of Your commandments, wherein
I take my delight.

May I set my heart
on the things that You teach me,
not on love of gain.

Turn my gaze away
from evil and foolish joys;
Your word gives me life.

Honour the promise
You have made to Your servant,
that all may dread You.

Avert from my head
the insults that frighten me,
out of Your goodness.

See, Lord, how I yearn
for Your life-giving precepts.
May they enrich me!

Waw   Your love never fails.
May it light upon me, Lord,
bringing promised help.

Then shall I answer
all who taunt and deride me,
for I trust Your word.

Never take from me
the joy of Your faithful word,
source of all my hope.

May I never fail
in the keeping of Your law,
now or forever.

Thus, true to Your word,
I shall follow where I will
the path of freedom,

making known to kings
without fear of disgrace
what You have taught me.

All Your commandments
have filled my soul with delight.
I dearly love them.

I stretch out my hands
to Your beloved precepts,
theme of my musings.

Zain   Remember the word
You proclaimed to Your servant,
basis of my hope.

Therein my comfort
in moments of suffering:
Your life-giving pledge.

The proud have mocked me
but I have unswervingly
cherished Your teachings.

I have borne in mind
Your rulings of other days
and in them found peace.

I seethe with anger
when I see how the wicked
abandon Your law.

To me Your statutes
are as psalms sung in exile,
ever in my mind.

In the dark of night
the very thought of Your name
binds me to Your law.

I can count myself
richly blessed in the keeping
of Your commandments.

Heth   Have I not resolved
to do all in my power
to live by Your word?

With all my heart, Lord,
I beg You to favour me
as You have promised.

Having considered
the course my life has taken,
I bow to Your law.

Without wasting time
I shall recommit myself
to Your commandments.

Though the snares of men
are waiting to entrap me
Your law holds me fast.

I rise in the night
to praise the righteousness
of all Your teachings.

People who fear You
and who obey Your teachings
are my dearest friends.

Your great love, O Lord,
is poured out over the earth.
Teach me Your statutes.

Teth   You have been true, Lord
to Your word, showing kindness
to Your poor servant.

Teach me discernment
and grant me clearer insight
whose trust is in You.

In earlier days
I wandered and went astray;
now I heed Your word.

You, O Lord, are good
and all that You do is good;
teach me Your statutes.

Though arrogant men
spread lies to blacken my name,
I keep Your precepts.

Gross their minds and hearts,
but I find all my delight
in Your holy law.

Affliction healed me
that I might be made aware
of Your statutes, Lord.

Your ordinances
are of greater worth to me
than silver or gold.

Yod   You, Yahweh, made me;
and You gave me the knowledge
of Your commandments.

When they look on me
those who fear You will take heart
and share in my hope.

Your decrees are just
so whatever afflicts me
is for my own good.

May Your love for me
always, as You have promised,
bring consolation.

Help me, Lord, to live
in Your tender compassion,
Your law my delight.

Put to shame the proud
who, while I muse on Your law,
seek to defame me.

Let those who fear You
and understand Your precepts
come to my defence.

Blameless be my heart
in its love of Your statutes,
with naught to shame me.

Kaph   With eager heart, Lord,
I await deliverance,
my hope in Your word.

My eyes are wearied
searching for what You promised.
Come to comfort me.

How long must I wait?
When will my persecutors
fall under Your ban?

Proud men dig pitfalls
in defiance of Your law,
seeking to harm me.

Come, Lord, to my help!
Fidelity to Your word
brought me to this pass.

In all they have done
I have never turned away
from Your commandments.

In Your steadfast love,
intervene on my behalf.
Save me by Your will.

Lamed   Eternal, O Lord,
unchanging in the heavens,
is Your holy word.

Lord, Your faithfulness
endures to the end of time
and the earth stands firm.

Your decrees hold fast
and, because all things serve You,
they will know no end

Your law delights me.
I would have died in my sins
had it not been so.

I shall not forget
the precepts which You gave me,
a true gift of life!

I am Yours alone
and know that my salvation
waits on Your precepts.

The wicked have plans
to bring me to destruction
but I seek Your will.

All things have an end,
but Your holy commandments
are boundless in scope.

Mem   How I love Your law –
the subject of my musing,
ever in my mind!

With Your commandments
I am wiser than my foes,
for they uphold me.

The insights they give
surpass those of my teachers,
for they fill my mind.

My understanding
is beyond that of the old,
thanks to Your teaching.

I shall never swerve
from the way of Your precepts,
from Your sound decrees.

Sweeter to my tongue
the promises You have made,
than choicest honey.

From Your wise teaching
I learn all that will keep me
from folly's false paths.

Nun   Your word is a lamp
casting light before my feet,
guiding my footsteps.

I have sworn an oath,
have taken a solemn vow
to live by Your law.

Deep my affliction.
According to Your promise
heal and console me.

Accept from my heart
the homage paid by my lips;
and teach me Your law.

At every moment
I take my life in my hands,
but hold to Your law.

Foes try to trap me
but I never turn my steps
away from Your path.

Your decrees are, Lord.
my eternal heritage,
the joy of my heart.

I shall give my life
to the keeping of Your law
to the very end.

Samek　How hateful are those
of divided allegiance;
I love Your teaching!

You are my refuge,
the shield that gives protection.
I hope in Your word.

Do not come near me,
you who engage in evil!
I keep God's command.

Be my support, Lord.
Do not disappoint my hope
that I shall be saved.

For my safety's sake
keep me, O Lord, ever true
to Your commandments.

You spurn all who stray
from the law set before them,
their cunning in vain.

The wicked, like dross,
You scatter in lost places.
I love Your decrees.

Before You, O Lord,
I walk in dread of judgement,
fearing Your decrees.

Ain   I have always sought
to do what is just and right.
You will not spurn me.

Assist Your servant
when he comes under attack
of his oppressors.

I look longingly
for Your saving help, O Lord,
Your promised justice.

Deal with Your servant
in accordance with Your love;
teach me Your statutes.

I am Your servant.
If You make it clear to me
I shall do Your will.

Now, Lord, must You act
for the law which You gave us
is being broken.

The Lord's commandments
are far dearer to my heart
than the finest gold.

Your precepts lead me
to paths of righteousness
I hate all falsehood.

Pe Your decrees so wise
my soul cannot but obey
with heartfelt respect!

Your light shines through them
so that even the simple
can grasp their meaning.

Panting open-mouthed,
I am thirsting and yearning
for Your commandments.

Show me Your mercy,
You who have such countless
lovers of Your name.

Make firm my footsteps
according to Your promise,
save me from all harm.

Look kindly on me
that I may be Your servant,
faithful to Your law.

Tears stream from my eyes
because there are so many
who flout Your precepts.

Sade How just You are, Lord,
and how truly righteous
are all Your judgements!

Just the instructions
which You impose upon us,
and utterly fair.

I am roused to wrath
at seeing Your enemies
neglect Your teaching.

All that You promise
has been frequently acclaimed
as worthy of love.

Though I be despised,
I shall never bring myself
to forget Your words.

Your righteousness
is eternal, unending,
and Your law steadfast.

Though grief and anguish
lay relentless hands on me,
Your law still gives joy.

Your ever just laws
arouse my heartfelt esteem,
giving me new life.

Qoph   With all my heart, Lord,
I call on Your holy name:
Help me keep Your law.

I cry for Your help
in the keeping of Your law.
Hear me and save me.

I rise before dawn
and, calling upon Your name,
put my hope in You.

All my long night hours
are spent in meditating
on Your promises.

In Your steadfast love
listen, Lord, to my pleading:
give me vibrant life.

I am surrounded
by men who wish to harm me,
men far from Your law.

Yet You are near, Lord,
and all that You have taught me
I know to be true.

I have long been sure
that Your decrees were founded
to last for ever.

Resh   Heed my suffering
and come, Lord, to rescue me
who follow Your law.

Uphold my just cause.
You promised to defend me
that I might have life.

There can be no help
for those who decry Your words
and go their own way.

Great is Your mercy;
according to Your rulings
grant me life, O Lord.

Though I am oppressed
by countless persecutors,
I swerve not from You.

Anger seizes me
at sight of the treachery
of base renegades.

Seeing how deeply
I love all Your precepts, Lord,
in love grant me life.

Truth is the essence
of Your righteous teachings,
now and forever.

Shin   Princes oppress me,
persecute me without cause;
Your law delights me.

I am jubilant
over Your promises, Lord,
like one who finds gold.

I have a hatred
for falsehood and delusions;
Your law is my love.

Seven times a day
I raise my voice to praise You
for Your sure teaching.

How great is their peace
who know and esteem Your law.
They never stumble.

My waiting for You,
is the observance, O Lord,
of Your commandments.

With a lightsome heart
I pay heed to Your teachings,
loving them dearly.

I obey Your will
and follow Your instructions
in the sight of all.

Tau   Let my cry, O Lord,
come to You in joyfulness;
enlighten my mind!

May my entreaty
be acceptable to You
and be my saving.

Let my lips gladly
make known my indebtedness
for Your sound teaching.

May my tongue make known
how just are Your promises
as it sings Your praise.

May Your hand be prompt
to come to my assistance
as I do Your will.

While I yearn, O Lord,
for the help You have promised,
Your law delights me.

Give life to my soul
so that, helped by Your decrees,
I might praise Your name.

I, like a lost sheep,
know You will seek Your servant,
who lives by Your law.

120

When, in sore distress,
I called to the Lord for help
He answered me.

"Lord, save me," I cried,
"from such untruthful people
and their faithless tongues."

How will He pay back
those purveyors of deceit,
enemies of truth?

With sharpened arrows
and by heaping upon them
the flames of His wrath.

Wretched is my lot:
exiled am I in Meshech
among Kedar's tents.

I have lived too long
among those who shout for war,
while I plead for peace.

If I raise my eyes
to gaze on surrounding hills,
shall I find help there?

My help comes only
from Yahweh, who made heaven
and created earth.

121

He will never let
my stumbling footsteps falter;
watchful, He sleeps not.

Israel's sure Guard
is One Who never slumbers,
never falls asleep.

The Lord is Your Guard
ever standing beside you,
keeping you from harm.

He is shading you
from the glaring sun of day,
from the moon by night.

The Lord will keep you
from every kind of trouble
and safeguard your life.

You are in His care
in your going and coming,
now and forever.

How great was my joy
when I heard them urging us
to go to God's house.

Now we are standing
before His very threshold
in Jerusalem.

New Jerusalem,
restored as the great city,
compact and solid.

There the tribes go up
in accordance with the Law,
to sing the Lord's praise.

The thrones of judgement
stand there – the royal tribunals
of David's proud house.

Jerusalem's peace
the theme of our petitions:
Long may it prosper!

Peace within its walls
and lasting prosperity
in its palaces.

My brothers and friends
are in my heart as I pray,
"Peace be among you!"

For love of God's house
I shall never cease praying
for its peacefulness.

122

I lift up my eyes
to You, enthroned in glory
in the high heavens.

As the eyes of slaves
fixed upon their master's hands;
or those of slave-girls

123

cannot turn their gaze
from the hands of their mistress,
so too are our eyes

fixed and riveted
upon the Lord our true God,
awaiting His gifts.

Show us Your favour;
we are treated with contempt,
scorn and mockery.

We are overborne
by ill-treatment and complaints,
scorn and derision.

124

Let Israel say,
"If the Lord our God had failed
to stand beside us –

if at that moment
when we came under attack
He had not been there,

then would we have been
swallowed alive by the foes
raging against us.

Then would the waters
have carried us right away;
we would have been drowned.

Blessed be the Lord
Who did not abandon us
as prey to our foes.

We, like threatened birds,
have managed to free ourselves
from the fowler's snare.

The nets being torn,
our struggles have succeeded
in setting us free.

We look to Yahweh,
maker of heaven and earth,
and never in vain.

Those who trust the Lord
stand as firm as Mount Zion,
quite unshakeable.

As Jerusalem
is protected by mountains,
so does He guard us.

125

Wicked men's power
cannot prevail for ever
against God's good friends,

otherwise the good
would have to use violence
to defend their rights.

Be good to the good,
to those who seeks to serve You
by their upright lives.

But evildoers,
those who walk by crooked ways,
drive them far away.

Peace on Israel!

When the Lord restored
to Zion its lost fortunes,
it seemed like a dream.

Laughter on all lips,
songs filling the hearts of all,
joy on every side.

The heathens exclaimed,
"The Lord is doing great things
for these, His people!"

What marvels for us
did He, the Lord, accomplish!
And how we rejoiced!

Deliver us, Lord,
from the bondage we have known;
bring streams to dry lands.

Crops sowed while weeping
will be gathered up in joy,
with laughter and song.

They went forth in tears
carrying their bags of seed;
harvest rejoicing.

Unless the Lord builds,
the masons will be toiling
vainly, without hope.

Unless He keeps watch
the sentries of the city
will guard it in vain.

127

Your early rising
and your late going to bed
serve no sound purpose.

Though you toil for bread.
It is the Lord Who supplies
food for those He loves.

Your very children
are gifts granted by the Lord,
your sons, His reward!

The sons of one's youth
can be likened to arrows
stored in a quiver.

How happy is he
whose quiver is full of them;
he will fear no foes.

128

How happy are those
who walk in fear of the Lord
and keep to His ways.

You will find pleasure
in the fruit of your labours
joy in possessions.

Your wife in your home
will be like a fruitful vine,
encircled by sons.

Such are the blessings
the Lord so willingly grants
to those who serve Him.

May He, from Zion,
give joy and prosperity
to Jerusalem.

May your life be long,
and may your children's children
gather around you!

From my youngest days,
this is Israel's lament,
I have been attacked!

From my youngest days
they harried and attacked me,
but have not prevailed.

My back, scourged by them,
is scarred and scored with furrows
like a well-ploughed field.

The Lord Who is just
has, in His righteous wrath,
freed me from their bonds.

Those who hate Zion
will, in shame and confusion,
be brought to nothing.

They will be like grass
that sprouts uselessly on roofs,
that earns no profit.

Not worth the reaping,
yielding nothing to binders
or to harvesters!

Those who are passing
will wish no blessings on them,
offer no greetings.

129

From out of the depths
I have called on Your name, Lord.
Listen to my prayer.

Give Your attention
to my cry of deep distress.
Unless You, O Lord,

130

show us the mercy
of overlooking our guilt,
how can we survive?

But You do forgive,
for which great act of kindness
we revere You.

My heart longs for You,
waits with greater eagerness
than watchmen for dawn.

Let Israel, Lord,
count on Your early coming
in unfailing love.

With You is mercy,
and generous redemption
from our many sins.

My heart is not proud;
nor, Lord, are my eyes haughty.
I am not embroiled

in things beyond me
or matters of great moment.
I have set my soul

on silence and peace
like a newly-weaned infant
at its mother's breast.

Look, O Israel,
have confidence in Yahweh,
now and forever.

131

132

Remember, O Lord,
the many adversities
endured by David;

how he swore an oath,
bound himself by solemn vow
to the Lord Most High:

"I will neither live
nor will I rest in my home
or let myself sleep

"until I provide
for the Lord, the Almighty,
a sanctuary."

We, at Ephrathah,
were given news of the Ark.
We came upon it

in the Forest Fields.
Let us enter His dwelling,
bowing before Him.

Arise, Lord Yahweh,
and come to Your place of rest,
the ark of Your strength.

Your priests shall be marked
by their robes of holiness,
Your devout by joy.

For Your servant's sake,
David whom You have chosen,
do not reject him.

The Lord swore an oath
in favour of King David,
which He will not break.

"A prince of your line
shall I set upon your throne
if My laws are kept.

"If your sons keep them,
their sons in turn for all time
will sit on your throne."

The Lord chose Zion,
selecting her for His home
and His resting place.

"This, my resting place,
will be My home for ever.
That is what I want!

"With food in plenty
she shall be blessed, and with bread
for all her needy.

"Her priests I shall vest
with salvation; her devout
shall ring out their joy.

"The stock of David
shall flourish there, preparing
for my Anointed.

"All His enemies
will be clothed in confusion,
while He will be crowned!"

How good and pleasant
to be living together
in brotherly love!

sweet is the odour
of fragrant oil poured on heads,
flowing over beards,

as on Aaron's beard
when the oil was running down
upon his vestments.

The dew of Hermon
appears to be falling
on Zion's mountains.

Thus then is the Lord
bestowing His rich blessing:
life for evermore!

Come and bless the Lord,
all who are called to serve Him
throughout the long nights.

Lift your hands up high
in the Lord's sanctuary,
bless His holy name.

134

May our mighty Lord,
maker of heaven and earth,
bless you from Zion!

Let us praise the Lord.
The name of the Lord be praised,
by you, His servants!

You who minister
within the house of the Lord,
the courts of our God!

Praise His great goodness;
sing psalms in praise of His name
to give Him pleasure.

The Lord has chosen
Jacob as His very own
treasured possession.

I know His greatness;
that He is our own true God,
high above all gods.

He does what He wills
in heaven and on the earth
and in all the seas.

He conjures up mists
summoned from vast distances
and makes lightning flash.

He calls forth the wind
from where it had been concealed
within His storehouse.

Egypt's first-born sons
of men themselves and their beasts
He struck down in death.

His signs and portents
wrought havoc throughout Egypt
and in Pharaoh's court.

He struck down nations
and the might of their armies,
slew powerful kings:

King Og of Bashan,
Sihon of the Amorites,
Canaan's kingdoms.

Their lands were granted
to Israel's own people
as a heritage.

All generations
will join in praising Your name
for ever, O Lord!

The Lord gives justice
and is filled with compassion
for all His servants.

The nations have gods
fashioned from silver and gold,
the work of men's hands.

Of what use are they,
with their mouths that cannot speak
and eyes that are blind?

Their ears hear nothing,
and their mouths are not able
to breathe in or out.

Soon will their makers
become the same as their gods.
Those too who trust them.

Israel, bless God!
House of Aaron, bless the Lord!
You, too, Levi's house.

Blessed from Zion
be He Who has His dwelling
in Jerusalem.

Praise the Lord.

Give thanks to the Lord,
His love is everlasting!
How great His goodness.

To the God of gods,
His love is everlasting!
give eternal thanks.

To the Lord of lords,
His love is everlasting!
our enduring thanks.

The One and Only,
His love is everlasting!
maker of marvels.

He made in wisdom,
His love is everlasting!
the mighty heavens.

He spread out the earth,
His love is everlasting!
upon the waters.

Maker of great lights,
His love is everlasting!
the sun rules the day,

moon and stars the night.
His love is everlasting!
give thanks to His name.

Who smote the first-born,
His love is everlasting!
of the Egyptians,

136

Who brought Israel,
His love is everlasting!
out from among them.

With His mighty hand,
His love is everlasting!
and His outstretched arm

He split the Red Sea,
His love is everlasting!
for His people's sake.

Pharaoh and his host,
His love is everlasting!
He swept to defeat.

Through the wilderness,
His love is everlasting!
He led His people.

He struck down great kings,
His love is everlasting!
slew mighty rulers.

Amorite Sihon,
His love is everlasting!
and Og of Bashan.

The Israelites,
His love is everlasting!
were given their lands.

Thus a legacy,
His love is everlasting!
came to Israel.

He kept us in mind,
His love is everlasting!
when we were in need.

He came to our help,
His love is everlasting!
when we were attacked.

To all He gives food,
His love is everlasting!
when they are hungry.

Give thanks to the Lord,
His love is everlasting!
the God of heaven!

137

We sat down and wept
by rivers in Babylon,
recalling Zion.

On the willow trees
that flourished all around us
we hung up our harps.

Our captors begged us
to sing them one of our songs
for their enjoyment.

"Sing for us," they urged,
"some of the songs you once sang,
those hymns of Zion!"

But how could we sing
one of the songs of Yahweh
in a pagan land?

Should I forget you,
beloved Jerusalem,
let my hand wither;

my tongue be silenced
if I were to forget you
even fleetingly;

or should I delight
in anything other than
you, Jerusalem!

Remember, O Lord,
what the sons of Edom did
to Jerusalem.

How they all shouted,
"Raze it to its foundations!
Bring it to the ground!"

Daughter of Babel,
blessed be he who treats you
as you treated us,

who seizes your babes
and, showing no compassion,
hurls them against rocks.

With all my heart, Lord,
I give You praise, Who have heard
the words of my mouth.

Before the angels,
in the heart of Your temple,
I bless and praise You.

I thank You, O Lord,
for Your faithfulness and love,
far beyond compare.

When I called for help,
You listened and You answered,
renewing my strength.

The kings of the earth
will join in thanking You, Lord,
for Your promises.

They pay Him homage,
gladly proclaiming how great
is Yahweh's glory.

The Lord, from above,
sees and cares for the lowly;
notes also the proud.

Though burdened by cares
and walking in affliction,
I am in Your hands.

You preserve my life;
to the anger of my foes
You give me Your hand.

Your stretched out right hand
will do everything I need;
is my salvation!

Your enduring love
will never abandon, Lord,
those whom You have made!

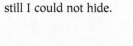

You are watching me;
whether I stand or I sit,
You know it at once.

You know all the thoughts
of my waking or sleeping,
and all that I do.

What I plan to say
is already clear to You
while yet unspoken.

You watch over me,
keeping Your hand upon me
at every moment.

Wonderful indeed
the knowledge You have of me,
far beyond my grasp!

Whither should I go
to escape from Your spirit,
flee from Your presence?

Climb up to heaven?
You are there! Sink down to hell?
There shall I find You!

Travel to the east?
Set off for the western bounds?
You would be my Guide!

If at my pleading
daylight itself became dim,
still I could not hide.

For to You darkness
is as bright as the daylight,
day and night the same.

It was You alone
Who created my being,
formed me in the womb.

It fills me with awe:
the wonder of my being
and of all Your works.

There are no secrets
of my body and my soul
hidden from Your gaze.

Your eyes beheld me
in the intricate weaving
that brought me to birth.

And into Your books
You marked the allotted days
that lay before me.

How precious to me
are Your thoughts of me, O Lord,
in all their vast scope!

To try to count them
would be like trying to count
sands on the seashore.

To finish counting
I would have to be like You
of age eternal!

Why, Lord, do You not
slay those who live wickedly,
shedders of our blood?

Men of evil will
who with malice defy You
and mock at Your name.

How I hate, O Lord,
those who hate and decry You,
who rise against You!

My hatred for them
is undying and boundless,
as for bitter foes.

Examine me, Lord;
gaze steadily at my thoughts,
test and try my heart.

Never allow me
to fall into wicked ways;
keep me in Your paths.

Rescue me, O Lord,
from the hands of the wicked,
men of violence;

men whose hearts are set
on cunning and wickedness,
stirrers up of strife.

140

Their tongues as deadly
as the forked fangs of serpents,
their lips drip poison.

Protect me, Lord God,
from the wiles of wicked men
who seek to harm me.

They plot my downfall,
and set, in their arrogance,
hidden traps for me.

I say to the Lord,
"It is You Who are my God;
have mercy on me.

"Strong to deliver,
You, O Lord, will shield my head
on the battlefield.

"Frustrate, Lord, the plans
of those who seek my downfall;
bring their plots to naught.

"Let my besiegers
see all their efforts thwarted,
their schemes overthrown!

"May red-hot embers
come raining down upon them
and all their helpers!

"Let them all be plunged
into rank and miry depths,
never more to rise!

"Slanderers will find
no one to give them welcome;
evils will hound them!"

I know that the Lord,
avenger of the wretched,
will right every wrong.

Good and upright men,
rendering their praise and thanks,
will bless Your presence.

I call to You, Lord;
come quickly and hear my plea,
pay heed to my cry.

Like smoke of incense
my prayers are wafted to You,
my hands uplifted.

141

Set a guard, O Lord,
at my mouth, and a watchman
in charge of my lips.

Never must my thoughts
dwell on things that are evil
nor plot wickedness.

Never allow me
to join with evildoers
nor share their delights.

Good men may strike me
or in kindness chide my faults.
Not so, the wicked!

I would not have them
anointing my head with oil!
Their evil scares me.

When they are brought low
with those who rule over them
they will understand!

Like shattered millstones,
their bones will be widely strewn
at the gates of hell.

On You, Lord Yahweh,
I trustfully fix my eyes,
counting on Your help.

Save me from the traps
wicked men have set for me,
from their poisoned bait.

Grant that the wicked
be ensnared by their own traps
from which I am spared!

I cry to the Lord:,
pleading aloud for His help
and for His mercy.

I pour out my needs,
make known to Him my troubles,
all that afflicts me.

142

When my spirit fails,
You keep Your eye upon me,
guide my every step.

They, my enemies,
have set hidden snares for me
wherever I walk.

To left and to right
I see no friends, no escape,
no one to save me.

I cry to You, Lord:
"In the land of the living,
You are my sole hope!"

Listen to my cry,
for I am completely crushed
by my foes' great strength.

Liberate me, Lord,
from my dire imprisonment,
that I may praise You.

In the Assembly,
with just men all around me,
I shall praise Your name.

143

Hear, O Lord, my prayer
and, in Your righteousness,
give ear to my plea.

Let not Your servant
(for who is pure in Your sight?)
be brought to judgement!

I was hunted down
by one who sought to crush me,
and thrown to the ground.

He forced me to dwell
in deep and deathlike darkness;
my spirit failed me.

I recall past times,
I think of all You have done,
my mind filled with awe.

I thirst for You, Lord,
as arid land for water,
lifting high my hands.

Lord, answer me soon!
If You hide Your face from me
I shall lose all hope.

In the morning, Lord,
let me know Your faithful love,
for I trust in You.

Make clear to me now
the way You want me to go
with heart fixed on You.

Save me from my foes.
To You I fled for shelter,
to be Yours alone.

May Your good spirit
lead my feet to level ground,
to ways that are smooth!

For Your name's sake, Lord,
revive and deliver me;
save me from distress.

In your love for me,
bring down all my oppressors.
I am Your servant!

144

Bless the Lord, my Rock,
He Who trains my hands for war,
fingers for fighting.

My Love, my Fortress,
my never-failing Helper,
my strong Citadel.

My Shield of defence
behind Whom I take refuge,
Who puts down my foes.

What then is man, Lord,
that You deign to notice him?
care to think of him?

His life but a breath,
his days a fleeting shadow
passing unnoticed.

Lower Your heavens
and come down, touch the mountains
that they pour forth smoke.

Send forth Your lightning,
flashing in all directions
like whistling arrows.

From on high reach out
and pluck me from deep waters,
from alien hands,

from the hands of men
whose every word is worthless
and all their oaths false.

I sing to You, Lord,
a new song – psalms to be sung
to a ten-stringed lute

in honour of Him
Who gave victory to kings,
Who set David free.

Save me from the sword,
rescue me from aliens,
lovers of falsehood,

those whose oaths are false,
whose every word is worthless,
steeped in perjury.

Our sons in their youth,
let them be like thriving plants.
And may our daughters,

like sculptured statues,
all be considered worthy
to grace palaces.

May our barns be filled
with all kinds of provisions;
may our sheep bear lambs

with our flocks growing
by thousands upon thousands,
and our cattle strong.

May cries of distress
no more be heard in our streets
and public places.

Happy the people
on whom are poured such
    blessings,
whose God is the Lord!

Aleph   I sing Your praises,
God my King, and for ever
bless Your holy name.

Beth   I, day after day,
shall praise and bless Your grandeur,
ever and always.

145

Ghimel   How great is the Lord!
Beyond man's understanding,
far beyond measure!

Daleth   One generation
will praise Your works to the next,
commend Your great deeds

Daleth   Men will tell the tale
of Your abounding goodness
with joy in their hearts.

He   How great Your glory!
I contemplate Your renown,
muse on Your greatness.

Waw   Your terrible deeds
will be on the tongues of all;
Your greatness on mine.

Zain   They will celebrate
Your overflowing kindness,
speak of it with joy.

Heth   Boundless His mercy,
His love-filled heart is tender
and slow to anger.

Teth He is good to all
and His compassion goes out
to all His creatures.

Yod All Your creatures, Lord,
render You their heartfelt thanks.
Your faithful bless You.

Kaph They shall speak, O Lord,
of Your kingship and glory
and affirm Your might.

Lamed May all mankind learn
of Your majestic glory
and Your mighty deeds.

Mem Your sovereignty
is eternal, Your kingdom
will last for ever.

(Nun) True to His promise
Yahweh always shows great love
in all that He does.

Samek Stumblers He supports;
should anyone bow you down,
He will lift you up.

Ain All eyes look to You,
and patiently You supply
their seasonal needs.

Pe Quick to satisfy
those dependent upon You,
You meet all their needs.

Sade   Ever righteous,
Yahweh's response to our needs
bears the mark of love.

Qoph   Yahweh stands beside
those who call to Him for help
with sincere hearts.

Resh   Those daunted by Him
need but to ask; He answers
ready to save them.

Shin   He gives protection
to the good; but the wicked
brings to destruction.

Tau   Blessed be Yahweh!
May He be blessed for ever
by all His creatures!

Praise the Lord

Praise the Lord, my soul.
I shall praise Him all my days,
always sing Him psalms.

146

Trust not in princes
nor in any mortal man;
they cannot save you!

They return to dust;
when their lives come to an end
their schemes die with them.

Happy is the man
whose hope is in Jacob's God,
Maker of all things:

of heaven and earth
and the sea, together with
all that they contain;

Who serves wrong doers
as deserved, but does justice
to the maltreated.

He feeds the hungry,
gives freedom to prisoners
and sight to the blind.

Those who are bowed down,
He delights in raising up;
and the just He loves.

He protects strangers,
supports widows and orphans
but thwarts the wicked.

He, the Lord, will reign
without end: your God, Zion,
from age unto age!

Praise the Lord!

Praise the Lord!

How lovely it is
to lift up Psalms to our God!
How good to praise Him!

The Lord Who rebuilds,
Who restores Jerusalem
and brings back exiles!

He is the Healer
of those whose hearts are broken;
he binds up their wounds.

He reckons the stars,
determining their number,
calling each by name.

Mighty is our God,
His wisdom beyond telling,
and awesome His name.

He, to the humble,
gives support; but the wicked
He casts to the ground.

O sing to the Lord
a glad hymn of thanksgiving;
with the harp, praise Him.

The sky He covers
with clouds, and thus provides rain
to meet the earth's needs.

He makes the hillsides
produce grass for the cattle,
shelter for nestlings.

Lord Yahweh's pleasure
lies not in a horse's strength
or a runner's speed.

He finds His delight
in those who accord Him fear,
who count on His love.

Sing hymns to the Lord!
Praise Him, O Jerusalem!
Zion, praise your God!

For He has strengthened
the bars of your enclosures,
has blessed your children.

He makes peace for you,
and supplies you with fine wheat
in great abundance.

He sends out commands
across the face of the earth;
naught can hinder them.

Snow as white as wool
He showers down upon you;
hoar frost like ashes.

He scatters hailstones
like crumbs till the waters freeze;
a word, and they melt!

He makes the winds blow,
and once again the waters
flow between their banks.

He makes His word known
to Jacob; to Israel
He gives His rulings.

This He does not do
for all the other nations
who know not His law.

Praise the Lord!

Give praise to the Lord!
From heaven sing His praises!
From the heights praise Him!

All angels, praise Him;
and praise Him too all His hosts;
praise Him, sun and moon;

148

Praise Him, shining stars;
and praise Him, highest heavens
and mists above them.

Let them praise His name
since it is by His command
they were created.

He established them
by His changeless ordinance,
for time unending.

Praise Him from the earth
you great monsters of the sea
dwelling in the deeps.

You, too, fire and hail,
snow and ice, gales and tempests,
pay heed to His voice.

All mountains and hills,
fruit-bearing trees and cedars,
obey His commands.

You, wild animals,
cattle and birds on the wing,
praise His holy name.

Princes of the earth,
all you rulers of the world,
young men and maidens,

the young and the old
let them all raise their voices
in praise of His name.

O praise the Lord's name,
that name unsurpassed on earth
or in the heavens.

He raised Israel
to lofty heights of glory
and crowns all His saints.

Praise the Lord.

Praise the Lord.

Raise up to the Lord
in His loyal assembly
a new song of praise.

Then will Israel
rejoice in Him Who made them,
Zion in their King.

Let them, with dancing
and instrumental music,
praise His holy name.

The Lord takes delight
in them, His chosen people;
He is their saviour.

Now may His servants
kneel before Him gratefully
singing songs of praise.

On their lips praises,
in their hands the two-edged sword
for wreaking vengeance

on heathen nations
which repulsed the Lord's approach,
and enslaved their kings.

False rulers enchained,
the Lord's trusted followers,
now richly repaid.

Theirs is the glory:
they execute the sentence
decreed by the Lord!

Praised be the Lord!

149

Praise the Lord!

Give praise to the Lord
in His temple on the earth
and in heaven's vault.

Praise Him for His might
and for His powerful deeds,
surpassing greatness!

Praise Him with fanfares,
with trumpet, harp and lyre,
tambourines and dance;

praise Him flute and strings,
praise Him triumphant cymbals;
clashing cymbals, praise!

May all that has breath,
praise and ever praise the Lord.

Other Seastone Titles

A.D. 1000: A WORLD ON THE BRINK
OF APOCALYPSE
Richard Erdoes
Introduction by Karen Armstrong
A chilling account of a chaotic time with un-
nerving parallels to our own, this book brings
us the life and career of Pope Sylvester II, a
visionary so brilliant many of his contempo-
raries assumed he had made a pact with the
devil. *Trade paper. $14.95*

AMERICAN INDIAN GENESIS
Percy Bullchild
Introduction by Mary Crow Dog
Written as it has been spoken for generations
in the Blackfeet style, this provocative work
provides a Plains Indian history of the world's
creation. *Hardcover. $16.00*

APOCALYPSE 2000:
THE BOOK OF REVELATION
John Miller, Editor
Introduction by Andrei Codrescu
Brings the fascinating Book of Revelation to
life with rich illustrations and modern reflec-
tions about the apocalypse by notable contem-
poraries. *Hardcover. $17.95*

BEFORE HE WAS BUDDHA:
The Life of Siddhartha
Written in a lucid, flowing style, this biographi-
cal profile reveals the strength and gentleness
of Buddha's character and brings to life the
compassion that gave his teachings universal
appeal. *Hardcover. $16.00*

DAVID: POWER, LUST AND BETRAYAL
IN BIBLICAL TIMES
Jerry M. Landay
The personal story of a man of ambition, com-
plexity, talent and human frailty, one of the
most popular heroes of the ancient world is
portrayed here with the care of a historian and
the color of a novelist. *Hardcover. $18.00*

DEAD SEA SCROLLS:
THE COMPLETE STORY
Dr. Jonathan Campbell
Dispels rumors surrounding the Scrolls and recounts the actual events of their unearthing, laying the groundwork for a vivid investigation of the relevance of the Scrolls to our times. *Trade paper. $12.95*

JESUS AND BUDDHA:
THE PARALLEL SAYINGS
Marcus Borg, Editor
Introduction by Jack Kornfield
Traces the life stories and beliefs of Jesus and Buddha, then presents a comprehensive collection of their remarkably similar teachings on facing pages. *Hardcover. $19.95*

MUSIC OF SILENCE
David Steindl-Rast with Sharon Lebell
Introduction by Kathleen Norris
A noted Benedictine monk shows us how to incorporate the sacred meaning of monastic life into our everyday world by paying attention to the "seasons of the day" and the enlivening messages to be found in each moment. *Trade paper. $12.00*

ZOO OF THE GODS: THE WORLD OF ANIMALS IN MYTH AND LEGEND
Anthony S. Mercatante
This fabulous bestiary reveals a wealth of tales from every culture, time and place. Underlying scores of animal stories are the relationships the author draws between beastkind and humankind. *Trade paper. $14.95*

To order these or other Seastone books call 800-377-2542, e-mail ulysses@ulyssespress.com or write to Ulysses Press, P.O. Box 3440, Berkeley, CA 94703-3440. There is no charge for shipping on retail orders. California residents must include sales tax. Allow two to three weeks for delivery.

FATHER RICHARD GWYN served as a
Brother of the Christian Schools from
1938 to 1978, teaching in London, Rome
and Canada. Since then he has lived at
the Cistercian Abbey off the coast of
Wales on the island of Caldey.